D1447293

BEL AIR
CHRONICLES

WITHDRAWN

3 1526 04306190 9

BEL AIR
CHRONICLES

CAROL DEIBEL

Foreword by MARYANNA SKOWRONSKI

Charleston London

THE
History
PRESS

Published by The History Press
Charleston, SC 29403
www.historypress.net

Copyright © 2012 by Carol Deibel
All rights reserved

Cover art by Alexandra Kopp, *Courthouse on Main*, www.alexandrakopp.com.

First published 2012

Manufactured in the United States

ISBN 978.1.60949.652.4

Library of Congress CIP data applied for.

Notice: The information in this book is true and complete to the best of our knowledge. It is offered without guarantee on the part of the author or The History Press. The author and The History Press disclaim all liability in connection with the use of this book.

All rights reserved. No part of this book may be reproduced or transmitted in any form whatsoever without prior written permission from the publisher except in the case of brief quotations embodied in critical articles and reviews.

Contents

CONTENTS

FOREWORD

The Town of Bel Air is not only the official county seat of Harford County, Maryland, but the historical one as well. It was the center of government and business even prior to its 1874 incorporation. However, not having the picturesque waterfront of Havre de Grace or the military significance of Aberdeen, the town has often been overlooked in terms of its historical and societal significance.

Author Carol Deibel's meticulous research shines a spotlight on Bel Air. What the town lacks in "picture postcard" real estate, it makes up for in life and personalities. Main Street's Governor Augustus Bradford Park marks the site where the home of Maryland's Civil War governor once stood. At the edge of town, one may visit Tudor Hall, home to the "first family" of the American stage—the Booths. At the turn of the last century, the town provided a sylvan summer retreat for Dr. Howard A. Kelly, one of the first department heads of Johns Hopkins School of Medicine. His Palladian mansion, the beautiful Liriodendron, now welcomes the public in its role as museum and cultural center. The Bel Air Racetrack provided sport and entertainment, as well as the site for the county fair. Bel Air was and still is the center of law and business in Harford. The oldest and most prestigious firms are headquartered in the town, and many of the shingles bear the names of descendants of the founders.

In the end, what makes this book so readable and so important are the many firsthand interviews that were conducted during its writing. The stories and anecdotes provide color and personality, breathing life into the facts. The shutters have long been closed on Bel Air's history. Carol Deibel has thrown them open. May they long stay that way!

Maryanna Skowronski
Director
The Historical Society of Harford County
June 21, 2012

PREFACE

Writing *Bel Air Chronicles* was truly a labor of love. After working in and for Bel Air for more than thirty years, I thought I knew its stories and wanted to share its legends with others. What I discovered in my research was a far richer, more complex history than I ever imagined. While this is in no way a comprehensive history of Bel Air, I hope these stories will entice you to explore its history, particularly its people and their adventures, and to better understand its journey from frontier to modern suburbia.

I need to thank many people who helped make this book a reality. First, Hannah Cassilly at The History Press, who took a chance on a first-time author and helped every step of the way, and the volunteers at the Historical Society of Harford County, Inc., who routinely provided news clippings, articles, photographs and background information from the society's vast archives and beyond. I also need to express sincere gratitude to two incredible Bel Air artists. The first is the cover artist, Alexandra Kopp, who took a very sketchy idea of what I hoped to illustrate and turned it into reality, and the second is Dave Gigliotti, a Bel Air photographer who provided photographs of the armory and patiently worked on the artist's photograph. I also need to thank my sons for guiding me through the numerous issues with the computer and picture scanning. Their technological expertise was invaluable. Without their patience and understanding, this book would never have seen the light of day.

Finally, I would like to thank my friends, who patiently listened to my stories and read the numerous drafts of each chapter for accuracy and content, and my family, for their patience as I disappeared for hours and hours of research, writing and editing. I hope you, the reader, enjoy the journey.

I

From Wilderness to County Seat

The Harsh Reality of Frontier Life

England's King Charles I, a friend of the Calvert family, granted Cecilius Calvert, the second Lord Baltimore, the land now known as Maryland in the 1630s. Lord Baltimore established the colony as a Palatinate, a form of government similar to the European feudal system. The Calverts hoped to replicate the landed aristocracy of earlier times. Based on this grant, the proprietor and General Assembly, composed of freemen or their delegates, could enact laws, punish violators in the province or on the high seas, take life or limb, confer dignities and tithes, raise and maintain a military force, wage war in the event of sedition or rebellion, proclaim martial law, establish ports of entry, impose taxes on merchandise, constitute manors, establish courts and barons, confer citizenship and trade with England and all countries with which it was at peace. Maryland's proprietary system gave ownership of the soil and complete jurisdiction over it to the Lord Proprietor himself, just as in a medieval fiefdom.

Anxious to establish his colony, Lord Baltimore began attracting colonists primarily from England. The high unemployment rates, periodic famines and depressions and an emerging European middle class, prohibited from purchasing land in England, helped his efforts. This New World opened up opportunities for prestige and property. The Calverts made the most of this, publishing broadsides extolling the

Cecilius Calvert, Lord Baltimore, the Lord Proprietor of Maryland. *Courtesy of the Historical Society of Harford County.*

colony as a "virtual Eden with food and livestock just for the taking." Some of the more outlandish claims included descriptions of parrots, oranges, gold, pearls and even peas that grew ten inches long in ten days. As further enticement, in 1633 the Lord Proprietor offered two thousand acres of good land and profits for anyone sending or bringing five men to take up land. Popularity of the offer quickly led to a modification, first to one thousand acres for every adventurer and then to one hundred acres per man, one hundred acres per woman and five hundred acres per child under sixteen.

The Palatinate charged an annual rent of twelve pence, similar to the ground rent still found in parts of Maryland today. By 1683, these inducements were unnecessary. New settlers paid two hundred pounds of tobacco for two hundred acres of land, tobacco being the main form of currency at the time. Upon arrival, all colonists took an oath of allegiance to the king. This was a way for Lord Baltimore, a Roman Catholic, to show his loyalty and was necessary because of the suspicion surrounding all Catholics in England.

The assembly, the colony's governing body, told colonists how to build houses and what to plant and advised them to avoid Virginia. Generally, there were two classes of colonists: gentlemen adventurers (mainly Catholics) and indentured servants (mainly Protestants). If a man could make a living without doing manual labor, he was considered a gentleman. An indentured servant was any person who contracted to work for a certain period of time in exchange for his passage to the New World. The contract for indentured servants in Maryland was usually for four to seven years and could be sold. There was also a third group among the early emigrants. These included low- to middle-class shopkeepers, artisans and a few farmers.

The journey from England was arduous, making it impossible for those in poor health to survive. Those who could afford the passage fee and survived the two- to three-month transatlantic crossing and the daunting prospects of finding shelter, fighting disease and establishing a farm were still plagued by isolation, the grueling daily routine of planting food and tobacco crops and the fear of Indian attacks. Even with such hardships, colonists continued to arrive, some escaping political upheavals in Europe and others fleeing for economic or personal reasons. As one colonist explained, "The world's in a heap of troubles and confusions and while they are in the midst of changes and amazes, the best way to give them the bag is to go out of the world and leave them."

The first settlers located along the shores of the Chesapeake from St. Mary's north to the mouth of the Susquehanna. The coastline, broken by frequent rivers and bays, about which were swamps and marshes, made communication other than by water onerous. Although George Alsop, who served Thomas Stockett as an indentured servant at Point Conquest in the 1640s, later wrote of the comfort and ease of life in the area, subsequent evidence does not bear out his reports. In truth, later journals indicated that the main body of settlers lived isolated, often primitive lives subsisting on wholesome but coarse food and strong drink.

New arrivals went to the secretary and keeper of the acts and proceedings of the Governor's Council to record their entry into the province and to establish their rights to land. These land grants often overlapped because of the surveying techniques of the time and the scarcity of surveyors. From St. Mary's, the colonists set out by boat with their limited possessions to find their allotted shelters and to clear massive first-growth trees to make way for essentials such as corn, peas and tobacco. Tobacco was essential because it was the main currency in the colonies. All salaries, fees, fines and taxes were paid in tobacco at first. It was also a highly labor-intensive crop that quickly depleted soils. Tobacco farming was ideally suited to the early settlements in southern Maryland, but the northern settlements lining the shores of the Bush River could not produce the same amount or quality of tobacco. The area did, however, offer fertile soils, abundant hunting grounds, fish and fur trading posts.

In 1638, four years after the settlement of St. Mary's City, Havre de Grace or Stockett's Town became the first settlement with any degree of permanency or legitimacy in Baltimore County, or what is today Harford County. This settlement was part of an area identified as Spesutia Hundred. A "hundred" was an English term initially designating a civil division for representation to the assembly. After 1654, it was also used to designate military and fiscal districts. Over time, the county included thirteen designated hundreds. The governor appointed a high constable, commander of the militia, overseer of roads and tobacco inspectors. The people of the hundred elected a tax assessor.

The original houses located along the shores were often cellar houses, very small, mostly wood. Generally, these were impermanent and could be torn down and moved as soil gave out. There were no rooms for specific purposes. By the end of the seventeenth century, styles changed. The assembly required more substantial buildings and towns. Settlers started using brick as well as wood. There was generally a keeping room, a hall that was the best room, a parlor used as a "borning room" or for courting and a separate building for cooking. The fireplace was at the center of the house and used fifteen to twenty cords of wood a year (about three acres). By our standards, the early colonists were young, small, tough, rum drinking and somewhat weathered looking. They died young and were often in poor health.

Before European settlers arrived, several Native American tribes lived and hunted in the area now known as Harford County. The

Ordinary howſes

A Susquehanna brave, as depicted on a map by John Smith in 1608. *Courtesy of the Historical Society of Harford County.*

Susquehannocks traded with the English, Swedes and Dutch settlers and, based on an agreement with Lord Baltimore, provided a frontier outpost to protect settlers from the Senecas, who repeatedly attacked early settlements along the Bush River. In 1630, the Susquehannocks numbered approximately 1,300. They were tall, well-built, industrious people who unfortunately had little resistance to diseases brought by the white settlers. By 1670, the tribe was reduced to about 300 people. Finally, in 1673, a war between the Susquehannocks and the Iroquois proved the final blow. Similar fates befell several other tribes who once hunted and farmed in the area.

A Shifting County Seat

The Maryland Assembly, attempting to ensure orderly settlement, ruled that the county seat for what was then Baltimore County be established on the west side of the bay. This provided good port access and a central location as the assembly confined all settlements to the shoreline for safety and accessibility, or as George Van Bibber explained in *A Trip to Old Baltimore and Other Points in the Bush River Neck*, "No wayfarer could venture into the unbroken forest to head the streams without risking his scalp." The forests surrounding the settlements provided wild game and fearsome adventures. This aboriginal forest enveloped interlopers with a darkness so deep no light could penetrate, even on the brightest days. Snakelike roots and years of debris lay on the forest grounds. Eerie sounds drifted through the woods, which harbored deer, bear, fox, rabbits, raccoons and other wild beasts. The shrill cries of birds, the hunted and the hunters, echoed through this unknown wilderness making every sound, every movement a potential threat. Still, the settlers came.

Initially, Baltimore County included present-day Baltimore, Harford and Cecil Counties. The assembly's first requirement for the county seat was the establishment of a court. Old Baltimore was located about a quarter mile from the elbow of Romney Creek on the site of what is now Aberdeen Proving Grounds. A courthouse, several taverns, an inn and a few houses stood near what was then a transatlantic port where cargo ships delivered and transported goods and ferries brought travelers from the north and south. This settlement was totally different from England or even New England. Settlers were cut off from daily contact with the world. The climate was similar to England's; the difference was the abundance of wood, fast-moving streams and limitless vacant land. Settlers girdled trees and used snake fences to keep animals out of gardens. Farmers shipped crops to English markets from the port at Old Baltimore and used "rolling roads" to bring hogsheads of tobacco from local farms to the port.

Once the settlement along Bush River filled up or became untenable due to depletion of the forest area and soils, settlers started moving inland along the streams and rivers. Settlers faced a stark existence compared to that in the home country. With no central village, they left behind holidays, traditional market days, festivals and most social gatherings.

Everyday routines revolved around work and family. Water was often unfit to drink, so early settlers depended heavily on hard cider and ale. Meals consisted of stew, milk and molasses. Pork was the primary meat, and settlers learned to eat beans, succotash, hominy and grits from the Native American inhabitants.

Baltimore County boundaries, which originally included present-day Harford and Cecil Counties. *Courtesy of the Historical Society of Harford County.*

In 1691, the assembly ordered that the county seat move to the confluence of the Little and Big Gunpowder Falls in the Gunpowder River estuary because silting at Old Baltimore's port limited use and access. Colonists prepared plans for the new town and requisite courthouse on the northeast side of the Gunpowder River to the west of Foster's Creek. Problems arose when Queen Anne refused to give her assent to the act creating the town. In 1709, the assembly directed that the site at Foster's Neck be abandoned and a courthouse be built on a tract, known as Taylor's Choice, belonging to Ann Felks. Thus, the county seat moved to Joppa. The Joppa area had the advantage of nearby quarries, allowing for construction of more stable stone buildings, a fine port and very fertile soils. Joppa quickly established itself as a port town and loading place, encouraging trade and ensuring prosperity. The town grew to quite a metropolis in the first half of the eighteenth century.

Joppa flourished for nearly sixty years, but just as silting of the earlier port in Old Baltimore forced the relocation of the county seat, silting at the Gunpowder became a major problem, and the assembly determined that the county seat should once again move, this time to Baltimore on the Patapsco. The county constructed a new courthouse on Calvert Street in what is now Baltimore City, and the deep-water port made it ideal for trade in tobacco and wheat. The county sold the Joppa courthouse and prison to help raise funds for the new Baltimore courthouse. The shift brought major discontent from citizens of the upper bay area. After five years, in December 1773, upper bay citizens submitted a petition to Annapolis requesting the establishment of a new county. To help substantiate the claims of the sixth Lord Baltimore, Frederick Calvert's illegitimate son, Henry Harford, to his father's property, the assembly chose the name Harford for the new county. Bush, a town established in 1683 along the Old Post Road, became the first county seat. As a sign of the times, even before construction of a courthouse began, local citizens adopted the Bush Declaration, a resolution believed to be the first Declaration of Independence ever adopted by any representative body in America. However, the population was moving inland, and people began to voice the need for a county seat located in the middle of the county.

Marker at the site of the former county seat at Bush. *Courtesy of the Historical Society of Harford County.*

This was not the first time that such a request was made. As early as 1686, Thomas Thurston petitioned the assembly

> *to appoint a place* [as the county seat] *where it may be set for the convenience of the whole county, which we do judge will be on the south side of the run called Winter's Run, convenient for every man that may have business there, which would be great satisfaction to the inhabitants and encouragement to travelers and strangers. Humbly desiring that the Council will grant our request:*
>
> *First: There is much land in breadth and length still to take up which is a great hindrance to the Proprietary.*
> *Secondly: There is many that have taken up land and are doubtful of seating because of fear of the heathen.*
> *Thirdly: It would be a means of driving back the heathen further into the woods.*
> *Fourthly: It will be near the middle of the county.*

Fifthly: The continuances of causes puts men at more charge than the debt, because that in the winter people cannot come for the frost, and here every man may come winter and summer.

Sixthly: It will be near the path that goes from the Potomack to the Susquehanna River and that will encourage strangers and enlarge our county.

This in behalf of the People of the Patapsco, Back River, Middle River, Gunpowder River and the south side of Bush River do request and Order of Council with what speed it may be and therein you will oblige the oppressed and promote the Proprietary Thomas Thurston

A NEW COUNTY/A NEW COUNTRY

On January 22, 1782, the General Assembly passed an act enabling voters of the newly established county to choose a new county seat. Choices included: Harford Town (Bush), Gravelly Hill, Lower Cross Road, Otter Point and Scott's Old Fields (Bel Air). At the same time, the assembly authorized justices to purchase four acres at the place selected and in the meantime to rent buildings for the courthouse and prison. Scott's Old Fields won the election, but Havre de Grace residents objected, and the assembly authorized a second election. The assembly explained:

> *Whereas sundry inhabitants of Harford County have petitioned this General Assembly for a law to remove the seat of justice from Bel Air to Havre de Grace and sundry other persons have demonstrated against the said petitions and prayed that the seat of justice therein should continue at the place already established by law; whereas, it appears to this General Assembly that the said dispute should be finally determined by an election of the people.*

The electorate again chose Bel Air.

The Town of Bel Air, laid out on lots that were part of Daniel Scott's land grant, Scott's Improvement Enlarged, consisted of a series of forty-two lots. In 1780, Scott's grandson, Aquila Scott, developed the original subdivision known as Scott's Old Fields from Scott's worn-out tobacco fields in an attempt to entice investors. On April 7, 1782, Aquila Scott conveyed by deed the lots for the courthouse, the jail and a sheriff's

Original plat for the Scott's Old Fields subdivision, later called Bel Air. *Courtesy of the Historical Society of Harford County.*

residence, just as William Osbourne had done one hundred years earlier at the first county seat, Old Baltimore. Initially, the justices held court in one of a row of houses that stood along the north side of Baltimore Pike (currently 220 South Main Street).

Citizens quickly determined that the name, Scott's Old Fields, should be changed. Thomas Hays, a prominent local landowner, one of those summoned by the legislature to sit on a delegation to determine the new name, helped to recommend Belle Aire as the new name. (Note the spelling. Over the years, several spellings appear. This was the original "French" version.) According to a letter from a cousin of Thomas Hays:

> *When the group learned that General Lafayette was coming through the newly constituted Harford County on his way to take part in the final battles of the Revolution terminating with the surrender of Cornwallis at Yorktown in 1781, they approached him with the news that they would name the new County seat after him. Lafayette expressed his gratitude but said that so many places had been named after him already and the end was by no means in sight. He begged the committee's indulgence and suggested that the town be named after a small manor belonging to him; among all the vineyards, chateaux and other feudal enclaves that were part of his estate; a spot where he loved to fish and hunt according to the season and the name of that place was Belle Aire.*

In 1782, Bel Air consisted of forty-two lots incorporating twenty-three and five-eighths acres overlooking Bynum Run. By 1798, the town had grown to include a jail, a courthouse and a few houses. Thereafter, the town grew incrementally to include hotels, bars, banks and many service businesses catering to surrounding farms and the business of government. The first lot was sold to Daniel Scott for thirty pounds in gold and silver. Other purchases soon followed, including one to John Love, Esquire, a delegate to the Annapolis convention in 1774; Gilbert

Jones, an innkeeper; Edward Robinson, a tavern owner; Benjamin Bradford Norris, one of the signers of the Bush Declaration; Robert Harris, a captain of Company I, the Flying Camp Harford Rifles; Jacob Norris, the trustee appointed to build the almshouse and an officer in the Revolutionary War; William Bond of Joshua, a member of the Revolutionary War Committee of Correspondence; Daniel Scott, the surveyor who laid out the courthouse lot in 1782 (also a signer of the Bush Declaration); Billy Drew Bunting, a widow and the only female lot holder; and Aquilla Standiford, a carpenter. The Act of 1784 confirmed the powers of the county commissioners and decreed that henceforth Scott's Old Fields should be known as Belle Aire. By 1798, the town boasted 157 inhabitants, a courthouse, a sheriff's house and jail and its first church, along with four licensed inns, three stores, two blacksmith shops, two joiners, one tailor, one chair maker, one shoemaker and one wheelwright. There were twenty-five houses, fourteen stables, four meat houses and one springhouse. The town was on its way.

II

Location, Location, Location

Hills and Valleys of the Piedmont

Bel Air offered many advantages as a county seat: a central location in the newly created county, numerous fast-moving streams, a relatively high elevation at the entrance to the Piedmont and strong local promoters. Transportation in the late 1700s was primitive at best. There were few bridges, so streams and creeks had to be forded. All travel was by water, on foot or on horseback. Roads were essentially old Indian trails or rolling paths created to move hogsheads of tobacco to market. The roads provided access to the mills, farms and customers of the merchants and peddlers packing their wares by horseback into the wilderness. Once the coastal waters silted in and the county seat moved to Baltimore on the Patapsco, the eastern part of the county lost much of its attraction. With concerns about the prevalence of malaria in the marshy areas of the county, the distance from inland settlements and the need for power to operate mills, Bel Air became a viable, even attractive, alternative.

Aquila Scott's entrepreneurial spirit also contributed mightily. Mr. Scott, the owner of Scott's Improvement Enlarged, could easily qualify as Bel Air's first major developer. Daniel Scott received the original patent for the land from the Lord Proprietor in 1701, expanding his holdings again in 1731. By 1745, at Daniel Scott's death, the property passed to his son James, who in turn bequeathed a portion of the property to his son Aquila Scott and the remaining land on the west side of what is now Main Street to his son Benjamin Scott. Benjamin sold his portion to William Bond, hence the development of Bond Street, a sixty-six-foot-wide public road laid out in 1817, and the Bond family's extensive development to the west of Bel Air reaching to Joshua's Meadows on what is now Tollgate Road.

Aquila recognized the opportunity for long-term profit in taking the old fields that were no longer viable tobacco fields and platting them as a town. In 1780, Scott platted forty-two lots along what was then the main road between Otter Point through Scott's Old Fields leading to the Rocks and the Pennsylvania line. The only other significant road at the time more or less paralleled Winters Run.

Many of the lands surrounding the town remained major farming centers for another two hundred years. Places like Majors Choice, Paca's Enlargement, Francis Holland's property and Joshua's Meadows provided part of the economic engine running the county's agricultural base. Aquila Scott's interest, spurred by his extensive inherited landholdings, led to several major land transfers. In 1775, he sold 103 acres of Beals Camp, located just outside the town limits, to William Smithson for sixty pounds current money of Pennsylvania. With the Revolutionary War on the horizon, currency was a tremendous problem. Hard currency was traditionally in short supply, and many transactions required a mixture of several mediums. There was no national currency, so financial transactions included currency from various colonies, later states, some British currency, gold and silver, as well as tobacco.

By 1782, Smithson's next purchase from Scott included 50 acres of Scott's Improvement Enlarged for £200. In 1790, Scott sold 65 acres next to the Smithson tract to William Maulsby, a blacksmith, for £440. Maulsby was the first recorded blacksmith in Bel Air but would be followed by many more. Among the first families in the central part of the county, the Scott family acquired over 2,300 acres of land between 1682 and 1741, much of this situated between Bynum Run and Winters Run, providing access to the Tidewater.

Water Power and the Confluence of Streams

In the 1700s, Winters Run and Bynum Run provided a means of travel, food, water and power to central Harford County. Before development depleted water levels with numerous wells and silting took its toll on these fast-moving, turbulent streams, they stretched across the county, drawing settlers with a promise of sustenance and readily available water power, the main source of energy at the time.

Today, the miller's importance to the community is barely understood, but in the early years of the colonies, a miller could make the difference between mere survival and prosperity. Grain was the primary food source. Colonists could grind grain each day with a mortar and pestle, a difficult and time-consuming process, or take their crop to a mill. Bel Air's location on two swift-moving streams made the mill industry in the area possible. Milling was a highly specialized craft, ideally combining the skills of carpenter, cooper, joiner, blacksmith and mason. Gristmills

Moores Mill, Bel Air's first gristmill. *Courtesy of the Historical Society of Harford County.*

required a large initial outlay of capital, since grinding stones had to be imported from Europe. Communities tried to lure millers by giving them a monopoly, offering them a choice plot of land and a royalty of 10 to 15 percent on a bushel of flour, treating the miller as a public utility. A good miller could judge the quality of grain by hand and eye, determining its age, moisture content and temperature, essential elements in determining proper stone speed. Some local mills also included tanneries and sawmills.

James Scott built Bel Air's first mill on Bynum Run between 1745 and 1747 on the land known as Scott's Close. This hundred-acre parcel provided the ideal location for a gristmill, immediately next to the stream and connected to Bel Air's main road through Major's Choice and what would later become Route 1. Scott built the initial dam and house, separate kitchen, stable, barn, sawmill and fencing, expanding his mill in 1762, essentially providing Scott with a monopoly on the gristmill business in the area. He sold the property to James Moores in 1773. Mr. Moores continued the gristmill, but as a tanner he also expanded the operation to include a tan yard. He used the sawmill for cutting and removing bark from the many oak trees on the property, grinding the bark with the millstones and placing it in a vat to tan the leather. Mr. Moores grew quite wealthy, enabling him to buy Paca's Meadows, William Paca's property, in 1780. The property, called Southampton, situated adjacent to the mill, brought his holdings to about 750 acres. The impressive brick mansion still situated on the site was built by Moores in 1780, housing his family until 1823, when James's son, John, died. Moores Mill operated continually for 132 years, at which time the millstone, which had been imported from Germany in 1745, broke. The ordinary life of a millstone was somewhat less than 33 years, making this a record-breaking millstone. Reports at the time indicated that the timbers were still sound and apparently good for another 100 years. With the development of electricity and the relative ease of transportation, the water-powered mill operations throughout the county declined at the beginning of the twentieth century. In 1928, Robert Heighe, a horse racing enthusiast, bought the property, demolishing the mill and building a large stone house. The old milldams became ice-skating ponds, and a way of life disappeared.

Once technology permitted, Henry Reckord built Bel Air's second and largest mill, Reckord's Steam Mill, on North Main Street in 1886.

Reckord Mill served Bel Air for more than one hundred years. *Courtesy of the Town of Bel Air.*

Town citizens donated the site for the mill conditioned on development of a plant with a daily capacity of fifty barrels of flour. At the time, it was considered "the largest roller mill east of the Ohio River." The building stood five stories, measuring forty by sixty feet, and included six double rollers, giving it a capacity of one hundred barrels, twice that required by the town. In 1894, the mill began to generate electric power on site. The generators provided power for the mill and power for the forty streetlamps of thirty-two candlepower that illuminated the town.

The mill underwent many changes during the last century, ranging from its major role as a stop along the Maryland & Pennsylvania Railroad to its role as a town public utility and as an electric generator. Today, it still functions as an agribusiness, although in a much different manner, catering to a very different clientele.

III

A COURTHOUSE TOWN EMERGES

MANDATES AND CHALLENGES

Harford County faced a daunting task in meeting the General Assembly's mandates for establishing a new county seat. Bel Air was a frontier town with a few houses, inns and taverns and not much else. The assembly ordered the county to build a courthouse and a prison and to establish a home for the poor. Funds were constantly in short supply, as were manpower, materials and expertise. Daniel Scott, who lived on Main Street next to the future courthouse, surveyed the courthouse and prison properties, which were transferred to the county in 1782; thus began a nine-year struggle to comply with state mandates as the country contended with even greater challenges in post–Revolutionary War America. Then, just as the county and Bel Air seemed comfortably established, the country was rent apart by the War of 1812 and then by a civil war, which tested loyalties and divided Bel Air in a way not seen before or since.

THE GENERAL ASSEMBLY DECREES

In 1773, the Maryland General Assembly established Harford as a new county, providing a series of mandates; appointing justices and a sheriff; specifying an election process; and specifying how and when a courthouse, prison and almshouse were to be built. The justices initiated purchase of two lots at the highest elevation in town from Aquila Scott of James. Funding for the land was provided from two sources. The assembly, in its Act of 1783, ordered the sheriff of Baltimore County to collect funds toward construction of the new county's government buildings, reasoning that Harford County residents paid toward the construction of the Baltimore Courthouse both in taxes and in the proceeds of the sale of the government buildings formerly in Joppatowne. Harford County residents were assessed 200,000 pounds of tobacco, which the Harford County sheriff collected. Baltimore's sheriff procrastinated, obviously not wanting to collect taxes for another county, until the assembly forced the issue by demanding full payment or forfeiture of Baltimore County's bonds. Construction began in 1788, but funds ran out before the courthouse was completed, so the assembly issued a second levy. The Act of 1790 assessed another £500, or two shillings, six pence per £100 worth of property, on Harford County residents to ensure completion of the government buildings. In the interim, court was held in rented buildings located near what is now the corner of Baltimore Pike and Main Street.

A Court, a Jail and a Home for the Poor

The name of the original courthouse and jail designer is unknown, but the courthouse was completed by James Johnson in 1791. Records show that he completed it "agreeably to the plan filed in the Clerk's office." The courthouse provided the focal point for all future development in Bel Air. The two-story brick building boasted a large courtroom housing the Petit and Grand Juries with a brick floor and two fireplaces, as well as a clerk's office and sheriff's office on the first floor. The second floor was reached via outside stairs. The jury room placed on the second floor was unheated, since the judges felt "a jury room should not be too comfortable." This area also held the commissioners' office and an apartment used by societies of the county and for holding village balls and the like. The court met in the new building for the first time in March 1791.

On February 19, 1858, disaster struck. At 4:30 a.m., flames burst from a second-floor window. The fire apparently caught from a stove in the county commissioners' office. Nearby residents rushed to the scene, but

Harford County Courthouse prior to the 1858 fire.

little could be done because there was no firefighting apparatus in the village. The fire burned furiously until 6:00 a.m. Fortunately for nearby properties, there was a severe snowstorm, which prevented the flames from spreading. Two wings of the courthouse survived the fire because the brick in these sections was covered with slate and protected with fireproof doors and shutters, thus saving birth, death and land records, but the court records were lost. Within days, the Maryland General Assembly introduced a bill authorizing construction of a new courthouse and a bond issue of $20,000. This time, construction proceeded quickly. The new courthouse was ready for occupancy in 1859. While under construction, the courts met in the Masonic Temple to the rear of the courthouse lot. The commissioners built the new courthouse in an Italian Renaissance style with rounded arches on both floors and Palladian windows. More richly classical additions followed in 1904, adding the east and west wings and the cupola. In an 1858 letter from county resident Abigail Carter to her brother, Levi Carter, she explains, "We are getting a new courthouse. They make us smoke it in taxes now a days. The tax gatherer's name is Amos Gilbert this year. He says he preferred gathering tax amongst the ladies—He says the gentlemen look awful hard at him for such enormous bills as he has to carry this season."

Building the required jail proved equally difficult. The Lord Proprietor appointed Thomas Miller as the first sheriff in March 1774. Two years later, the court held the first election, in which John Taylor, Esquire, defeated George Bradford, Esquire, to become the first elected sheriff of the county. The assembly established the sheriff's salary at 5 percent of the taxes he collected. His duties varied greatly from those today. He was responsible for collecting taxes, generally in the form of tobacco, which he then had to sell, distributing the proceeds to the building of the courthouse and prison and caring for any prisoners. Additional duties included apprehending malefactors; posting notices of elections; distributing and collecting ballot boxes; posting a constable, special deputy or election deputy at each polling place; ensuring that roads were kept in good repair; and overseeing any executions.

In 1804, the sheriff presided over his first execution. The Harford County court convicted a young black man, named Leander, of murder and arson. The victim was an elderly colored woman who sold cakes and beer from her home just north of Bel Air. Leander, with the assistance of an old black man, murdered her for her money and then set the house on fire. The accomplice turned state's evidence, leading to Leander's conviction. The sheriff arranged for the hanging to take place on Tulip Hill, near the Dallam property on North Main Street. A horizontal limb of a large chestnut tree served as a gallows.

By the mid-1800s, the sheriff's duties had changed. The assembly no longer required him to collect taxes, and it established a set salary. Still, the duties could be quite onerous. The assembly also provided strict specifications for construction of the first prison. It was to be thirty-five by thirty feet with two-foot walls built with stone and lime and a cellar under the entire building. One-quarter of the cellar was to be arched for a dungeon. The cellar must have seven-foot ceilings and the two upper floors, eight-foot ceilings. The lower rooms were to be lined with two-inch oak plank, well spiked and lathed with rough plaster or planks. The details went on to include roofing materials, the number of windows, type and size of doors, fireplaces and flooring. In 1787, the sheriff hired John Taylor to build the jail according to these plans. Taylor was unable to complete the job on time, so the sheriff hired John Moores in September

1791 to finish building the jail for an additional £285. At this time, the sheriff maintained a separate residence but based on an act passed in 1819, he was required to reside in the jail or to hire a resident jailer; otherwise, he faced a two-dollar-a-day penalty. The sheriff's house was built on the lot in 1819 to meet the conditions of the act. In the 1960s, the county demolished the buildings to make way for the county office building and jail at 45 South Main Street.

FROM JUSTICES TO COMMISSIONERS

In 1828, justices relinquished many of their duties to elected officials. The elected officials included five county commissioners, the sheriff, a state's attorney, a clerk of the court and a register of wills. The assembly also appointed three judges: John Love, William Webb and Aquila Hall.

The Board of Commissioners' new duties included making laws, levying taxes, providing for the health of the poor, fixing tavern rules, supervising the construction of roads, paying bounty for capturing wild animals, appointing tax collectors and apportioning funds for schools, courts and public facilities. The commissioners served four-year terms and ranged from three to five members. Initially, the county held elections at the courthouse, but once Bel Air became the county seat, the commissioners changed this, dividing the county into five districts so voters no longer had to come to the county seat. Voters received a ballot at the district office listing the candidates. A voter would scratch off any name he did not want to vote for. Elections tended to be rowdy affairs.

The Maryland Assembly required each county to establish a committee known as Trustees for the Poor, which was to purchase, maintain and manage poor farms or almshouses and to buy a tract of land not to exceed one hundred acres, build a house thereon and take care of "vagrant beggars and other indigents." Those able to work were kept at labor, and an overseer enforced the assembly's strict regulations. The overseer ensured that each inmate wore a badge with a large "P" on the right shoulder, together with the first letter of the county, cut in red or blue cloth. Refusal to wear the badge caused the subsistence to be withdrawn, and in obstinate cases, a vagrant was whipped not exceeding twenty lashes or given twenty-one days at hard labor.

The first almshouse, located near what is now Shamrock Park.

In 1767, the Levy Court granted funds to purchase a farm in the county seat not to exceed 50 acres. Twenty years later, Harford County commissioners finally appointed the required seven-member panel, the Trustees for the Poor, who purchased 50 acres from Aquila Scott on part of what is now known as the Shamrock Park development, near the present Bel Air Town Hall, at a cost of £200. The entire tract was sold at auction in 1831 to Reverend Reuben H. Davis, the first principal of Bel Air Academy. It became the home of Reverend Davis and his new bride, Mary Hays, the daughter of Archer Hays. The almshouse farm then relocated to Tollgate Road on a 256-acre farm south of Bel Air, where it operated until 1962. The land is now part of Heavenly Waters Park.

SNAPSHOT OF EARLY BEL AIR

For most of the eighteenth and nineteenth centuries, Bel Air remained a small village with two primary streets, Main Street and Bond Street. It was surrounded by a comfortable agricultural community on all sides.

A Courthouse Town Emerges

The Fernandis family played a prominent part in Bel Air from the early days through the Civil War era. *Courtesy of the Historical Society of Harford County.*

The Smithson farm, later owned by the Fernandis family, was south of town and included a Georgian mansion. The Boarmans and Bradfords also owned substantial farms south of town within walking distance of their Main Street homes, very similar to the European model of a central village surrounded by farms. In 1910, Harry and Hazel Hanway formed the Kenmore Farm Company and purchased a total of 568 acres of land along both sides of Emmorton Road from the corner of Main Street and Baltimore Pike south toward the Van Bibber B&O Railroad station, thus consolidating these family farms. Approximately 400 acres came from William Bradford and 68 acres from George Bradford. The Hanways also purchased 97 acres from Frances Boarman and 2¾ acres from Georgia Jacobs, along with numerous cows, heifers, bulls, horses, a sow and pigs from the various farms. The transfer documents included one McCormick mower, two corn workers, one lime sower, two dozen milk cans, one hundred barrels of corn, 175 bushels of oats, one milk wagon, one farm wagon, one truck, twenty-five tons of hay straw fodder and one hundred tomato cages. To complete the purchase, the Hanways bought a ½-acre piece, known as the old Bryarly property, which fronted on Main and Baltimore Pike, from the five Munnikhuysen sisters. Kenmore Farms became the home of a major dairy farm operation and the Kenmore Inn, one of the most successful hotels in the area until it was demolished to make way for a supermarket in the 1960s. The Bond family held similarly large farms and orchards to the west of Bond Street. To the east were several holdings of the Scott family and the 600-plus-acre Majors Choice land grant. Numerous smaller farms and orchards dotted the area north of town. A number of free blacks and slaves lived in this northern section and worked the surrounding farms.

Famous Residents

Many early inhabitants went on to important positions locally and nationally. William Pinckney, who lived in a house at the corner of Baltimore Pike and Main Street, later the location of the Kenmore Inn, went on to pass the bar in 1789 and become the U.S. attorney general. Thomas Hays, his next-door neighbor, served in numerous capacities in government at the state and local level and is credited with naming the town. In 1818, he was appointed quartermaster of the Fortieth Maryland Military Regiment, a precursor of the Maryland National Guard. He was one of the largest landholders in the area, owning fifteen of the original forty-two lots that made up Bel Air. He owned several businesses, residences and farms amounting to approximately four thousand acres. The Hays House is now a museum featuring historic reenactments and telling the story of the early days of Bel Air and the colony. It is not located at its original site but nearby.

William Pinckney (March 17, 1764–February 25, 1822) was an American statesman and diplomat and the seventh U.S. attorney general.

Another early resident who went on to become a state official was Augustus Bradford, who served as Maryland's governor during the Civil War. Governor Bradford was born in 1806 in a brick and frame house located at the corner of Main Street and Churchville Road. In 1835, he married Elizabeth Kell. Together they had twelve children. After leaving school in Bel Air, he went to Saint Mary's College in Baltimore to study law under Otho Scott. Admitted to the bar in 1827, he practiced law in Bel Air until 1831. The family moved to Baltimore for a short time and then returned to Bel Air to protect their children from an outbreak

Thomas Archer Hays (1780–1861) was a prominent Bel Air attorney and property owner and quartermaster of the Fortieth Maryland Military Regiment. *Courtesy of the Historical Society of Harford County.*

of cholera. In 1838, he returned to Baltimore and lived there for the remainder of his life. He was originally associated with the Whig Party but joined the Union Party in 1861, when he was elected as Maryland's governor. His term as governor was tumultuous. As a slave owner and father of a Confederate officer, he was in a very awkward position. After his own slaves escaped to Washington, D.C., he protested to President Lincoln that the district failed to uphold the 1850 Fugitive Slave Act—to no avail. He feared that calling out the state militia to protect slavery would lead to a disastrous clash with Federal troops, so he determined that the state had to accept the losses as a cost of war, angering many of his constituents.

Early Industry

In the early days, travel was extremely burdensome, so those with business at the courthouse stayed overnight in Bel Air, leading to a proliferation of inns and taverns for the travelers' entertainment. The Eagle Hotel was the earliest, built in 1718 of squared weatherboard covering an underlying log cabin. The hotel was situated on Bond Street west of the

Eagle Hotel, built in 1718, was the earliest hotel in Bel Air and was later known as the Country Club Inn. *Courtesy of the Historical Society of Harford County.*

courthouse. With growing demand, the Eagle expanded many times and was eventually renamed the Country Club Inn (1930). By 1820, at least three more inns were in place: McIlhenny's, next to the courthouse on Main Street; the Union Hotel, operated by Thomas Hays on Baltimore Pike and Main Street; and Gover's Inn, which occupied the impressive house built by Robert Nesbitt at Main Street and Courtland Street. This hotel, operated by Justin Moore, had a piazza across the front and a garden and stable for the guests in the rear of the building. Many inns and taverns followed as the county expanded. With this growth came more and more residents and new schools, churches and stores.

Town Institutions

Many of the local churches owe their beginnings to the Masonic Lodge. In 1826, the county conveyed a portion of the courthouse property to Mount Ararat Lodge #44 to build a building for public worship and a

The Masonic Lodge served Bel Air citizens as a meeting place, house of worship for many denominations and community center throughout the nineteenth century. *Courtesy of the Historical Society of Harford County.*

Masonic Hall. The church and hall opened in 1830, situated just west of the fence surrounding the courthouse property. The lodge met on the second floor. Various denominations held church services downstairs. This required careful scheduling. In 1886, with the permission of the Maryland General Assembly, the Masons replaced the building with a second larger and more elaborate temple built by Jacob Bull. The new structure provided community space for dances, cultural activities classes and government services. The Masonic Temple was demolished in 1980 to allow for expansion of the courthouse, eliminating one of Bel Air's most impressive structures.

Several local churches met at the Masonic Lodge until congregations became financially sound enough to construct churches of their own. The Presbyterian Church was the first to leave, building its church in the Greek Temple style on Pennsylvania Avenue. The Methodists built a new church on Main Street in 1856, and the Emmanuel Episcopal Church followed in 1870. The Masonic Lodge remained the center of town cultural activities well into the twentieth century, replacing the church services with dances, concerts and cultural events.

Now the Odd Fellows Hall, this was originally the first home of Bel Air's Presbyterian Church. *Courtesy of the Town of Bel Air.*

The original Emmanuel Episcopal Church, built by Jacob Bull in 1868, was redesigned and enlarged in 1894 by the Baltimore firm Wyatt and Nolting to meet the expanding needs of its growing congregation. *Courtesy of the Town of Bel Air.*

Schools in the early days were generally private, often beyond the means of the average citizen. As early as 1811, by an act of the General Assembly, plans began for the Bel Air Academy on Pennsylvania Avenue. The school opened in 1814, providing a classical education exclusively for boys. The state initially provided a $500 grant, but students had to pay tuition and board based on the studies selected. Fees began at $50 per term for board and washing. Classes in English were $12 per term; they were $10 per term for French and $15 per term for classics. There was also a set charge of $1 for stationery. An advertisement in 1841 went as follows: "Bel Air is a village of 25 or more houses, six taverns and the Academy has 100 students." The curriculum served those wishing to enter the professions.

There were other schools in the town; one boarding school run by a Quaker widow, Mrs. Cloud, was on Main Street near the courthouse. She, along with two other teachers, taught needlework, painting and general studies to day students and boarders. In 1870, Herman Stump Jr. deeded a lot at the northern end of Main Street where Bond Street and Main Street meet for development of a public school. John Lingan built a one-room school on this site. Teachers divided the pupils into three classes: primary, those in a speller or first reader; intermediate, those in a speller and second reader; and third class, those commencing to write in a copybook. Pupils purchased their own textbooks and paid tuition of forty cents for first term, seventy cents for second term and one dollar for the third. The state did not abolish the fees until 1916. The state paid teachers four times a year based on the enrollment. Again, this changed in 1916.

The remainder of the town included Courthouse Square with its attorneys' offices, a few residences and local businesses. Several blacksmiths, surveyors, wheelwrights, shoemakers, chair makers, a stagecoach office and stores of various types graced Main and Bond Streets.

TURNPIKE PLANS PROCEED

With the growing number of residents and the need for better means of transportation, local residents petitioned the state to allow development of a turnpike between Baltimore and Bel Air. The Act of 1815 provided approval "to make a turnpike or artificial road from the City of Baltimore to the site of the Susquehanna Bridge near Rock Run. The County was empowered to run this road through Belle Air."

Work started in Baltimore in 1816 but proceeded very slowly. The turnpike differed from other roads at the time by the fact that it was built of stone hauled from the surrounding countryside and crushed with small hammers by slaves or cheap laborers. The investors sold stock in the road and ran lotteries to meet costs. Thomas Hays, one of the managers and an investor in the turnpike, purchased stock contingent on the road going past McIlhenny's Tavern on Main Street rather than taking the originally planned route along Bond Street. Mr. Hays was one of the owners of the tavern. The investors expected to receive a return on their money through the tolls charged for use of the road. Plans included a tollhouse at Baltimore Pike and Tollgate Road, where fees established by the state could be collected. State law required that a rate table be posted

The tollhouse originally served as a collection point on Baltimore Pike. It was destroyed by a bomb that detonated prematurely when supporters of H. Rap Brown, a civil rights activist, sought to blow up Bel Air's courthouse before his trial in the 1970s. *Courtesy of the Historical Society of Harford County.*

for travelers to see. Typically, rates ranged from two cents for a small wagon to twelve cents for a score (twenty) of cattle or a stagecoach.

By 1820, the road was still just ten miles outside Baltimore. By 1830, it was still not past the Gunpowder River. Finally, in 1857, Harford County investors decided to build westward to meet this road from Baltimore (the current Harford Road), at last completing the turnpike.

CIVIL WAR DIVIDE

The town expanded, providing services for the outlying agricultural community and growing as a business, government and cultural center for the county. Still, there were many divisive political undercurrents that would soon wrench the community apart. As early as 1826, Baltimore County petitioned for a law that would "eventually but gradually and totally extinguish slavery in Maryland." Baltimore City and Harford and Frederick Counties submitted similar petitions, all unsuccessful. This by no means showed universal support for the abolition of slavery in Harford County. By the mid-1850s, national concerns about states' rights and slavery festered locally. A new political party, known nationally as the Know-Nothing Party, established its Harford County chapter. The group espoused a creed embracing two principles: hostility to new immigrants (particularly Irish Catholic ones) and opposition to slavery's expansion into new territory. John Wilkes Booth, a local resident, joined the fledgling political party, somewhat enamored by the fraternal organization's clandestine passwords and private rituals. Members joined by invitation only. Meetings were held in hidden locations, and those pledged to the brotherhood swore a special oath of allegiance, avowing that they were native-born citizens and Protestants and that they were not united in marriage with a Roman Catholic. Booth, sixteen at the time (1854), was tapped to carry a banner at a rally for Henry Winter Davis, a Know-Nothing candidate for Congress. Considered a remarkably handsome young man, Booth cantered down Hickory Avenue in party colors toward the speaker's platform where, according to his sister Asia Booth Clarke in her book, *The Unlocked Book*, his horse suddenly plunged into a roadside ditch, spooked by its rider waving a flag. Booth leaped off, hoisted the colt and, by aid of the flagstaff and without touching the stirrup, sprang lightly into the saddle and dashed off again, looking back with a reassuring smile. This remarkable agility later played a part in the assassination of President Lincoln.

County residents' sympathies remained split between the Union and Confederate causes throughout the war years. Accusations flew in all directions about the elections, both for the president and the governor. Tensions remained at a fever pitch as Marylanders debated remaining with the Union or seceding. When Governor Bradford took office in 1861, his status as a hometown boy did not carry much weight. He was fifty-five years old at the time, a lawyer and a slave owner, but he believed that the rebellion should be suppressed by force if necessary. Many in Bel Air and Harford County belonged to the States' Rights Party and generally supported secession and the war.

The two local Bel Air newspapers became the voices for the opposing sides. The *National American*, published by Richard E. Bouldin, son of the local sheriff, strongly supported the Union, while the *Aegis*, which was published by John Cox, was described by a Baltimore paper as "the *Traitor Aegis*." Issues continued to accelerate in 1862, when even many pro-Union supporters worried that abolition of slavery would become law and that many local citizens were being held prisoners solely for opinions, not actions. President Lincoln had suspended the writ of habeas corpus, allowing this detention early in the war. In February 1862, the president

Augustus W. Bradford was born at his family home on Main Street in Bel Air in 1806. He served as Maryland's governor from 1861 to 1865.

ordered the release of those prisoners who swore not to support the Confederacy. This brought some Confederate sympathizers back from Canada, where they had gone to escape arrest.

As an example of the bias of the *Aegis*, it reported on the military occupation in Bel Air in July 1861 as follows:

> *The dull monotony of our quiet little village was somewhat disturbed on Saturday morning last by the entrance into it of some two or three hundred half-starved, ill-clad, wo-begone looking wretches, carrying Minnie muskets, and commanded by officers of the 12th Regiment Pennsylvania volunteers. They were marched into town about 4½ A.M. by a guide named March McComas, and came from the neighborhood of White Hall, on the Northern Central Railroad, from whence they marched, under cover of the night, a distance of twenty to twenty five miles.*
>
> *Before entering the village, probably expecting an attack from the "rebels," they threw out their pickets upon all the roads surrounding the town, when the main body entered and stacked arms in the square fronting the courthouse.*
>
> *As soon as the great body of the "braves" had secured themselves comfortable quarters for a snooze—some along the curbstones, and others on the porches of the hotels and dwellings etc.—guards were dispatched to the residences of Captain Archer H. Jarrett of the Harford Light Dragoons, and Henry D. Fernandis, Esq. who were each brought into town as prisoners of war. A demand was made of Captain Jarrett for the arms of his company, purporting to come from Major General "Union-Sliding" Banks and upon failing or refusing to hand them over he was detained as a profiteer and taken to Cockeysville from whence he proceeded to Baltimore and returned to Bel Air on Sunday, having been released upon his parole.*
>
> *...Several little incidents occurred during the "military occupation" of the town which served to impress its inhabitants with the dignity and self importance with which these valiant soldier boys enforced their "military rules"...On approaching one of the houses doomed to be searched, they were met by the ladies, who inquired by what authority they intruded themselves into their presence. The officer informed them that there were concealed arms in the house; which charge was denied, and admittance refused. The captain ordered the soldiers to be seated*

in the piazza while he sued for admittance. One of the ladies informed him that there were no arms in the house belonging to the Government. When she was called to mind that there was one gun, which she had forgotten—the eyes of the soldier sparkled with delight at this piece of good news. The lady entered one of the rooms and returned with a small wooden gun, the toy of a small boy, and begged them to accept it, if it would be of any service in defense of The Capital or the preservation of the Union. The officer was greatly confused on the presentation, and still begged to search. One of the ladies requested him to clean his boots, and he could come in. He walked into the parlor, sank into the first seat visible, and appeared deeply sensible of the impropriety of his mission.

Soldiers searched the homes of Henry Fernandis, Esquire, and Thomas A. Hays, Esquire, and the county jail for arms. They forced the door of the town hall with an axe but found only a half dozen cap boxes, an unserviceable gun belt and a bullet mold. The soldiers behaved very gentlemanly, according to local residents. While the town was "under siege," no one was allowed to leave. Citizens complained that they were unable to bring their cows in from pasture. A number of Negroes joined the Union army before they left. The newspaper reports were clearly slanted to the bias of the paper at that time, noting that the "Negroes would be denied the privilege of returning to the bosoms of their friends and families until the close of the war." With the exception of this incident, the town was not involved directly in any battles or occupations during the war, but families were severely strained.

On March 15, 1862, John Cox resigned from the *Aegis*, noting his disappointment with the Union support in Harford County and the political situation in general. Alfred Bateman, a local attorney, took over the paper and added a motto: "The Union—It must be preserved." The motto was dropped after the first issue. Interestingly, both papers included scathing editorials in April 1862, dismissing the congressional legislation authorizing the Federal government to compensate any state that abolished slavery.

Meanwhile, public sales of slaves continued at the courthouse door as the Civil War raged. Approximately two thousand slaves were sold in Harford County between 1775 and 1863. Maryland law regulated slavery, often with cruel and onerous requirements. There were different rules for mulattoes and Negroes. The punishment for intermarriage required a Negro to be sold into slavery for life and the white person to serve seven years in indenture. The state had separate laws for Negroes and whites. Crimes ranged from lying to murder, and punishment included whipping and mutilation (such as cropping ears and chopping off a hand). For more serious infractions, the punishment was death. Neighbors and family members conducted many slave sale transactions privately; others occurred due to sheriff's sales, seizure for failure to pay taxes and the like. The prices varied widely depending on individuals (i.e., relatives or friends might make sales for token amounts). The

5 NEGRO MEN
FOR SALE.

BY VIRTUE of an order of the Circuit Court for Harford County, I will sell at Public Sale,

On Tuesday, the 22d

Day of June, 1858, in the town of Bel Air, five stout, healthy negro men—one for the term of 14 years, to be removed beyond the limits of the State of Maryland; one for the term of ten years, to be removed beyond the limits of the State of Maryland; and three for the term of five years each. These negroes are all good farm hands. They will positively be sold on the above named day to the highest bidder for Cash.

MICHAEL WHITEFORD,
ju5   Sheriff of Harford County.

The sale of slaves continued from the courthouse steps until 1863. *Courtesy of the Historical Society of Harford County.*

price for men, women and children also varied by age and sex; often the sale was for a limited time. Because slavery was illegal in Pennsylvania, slaves were leased in Harford County to avoid state laws. After the War of 1812, increased labor demands for growing cotton plantations in the Deep South brought slave buyers to Harford. Baltimore slave buyers advertised liberal prices for Negroes and indicated that they were the largest dealers engaged in the trade. They were always buying and shipping to New Orleans. A few buyers from New Orleans appeared in Bel Air looking for "special goods" between 1817 and the 1830s.

In 1752, Maryland adopted a law allowing manumission of slaves, but this included numerous conditions. A slave could only be freed if the owner was free of debt and had two witnesses to the manumission. A slave must be under fifty years of age and able to live by work. The age was later changed to forty-five; apparently, this was not strictly enforced because records show several slaves manumitted at age sixty and older. But manumission remained the exception rather than the rule.

The war years tore the community apart in many ways. Being a border state with a history of slave ownership, families were drawn in different directions. One of these families, the Bissells, owned the Gover Hotel on Main Street when the war started. Mr. Bissell was born in Virginia in 1811 and was a carpenter by trade. His wife, Margaret, was the daughter of John Adams Webster. She was born in Harford County in 1817 and grew up on the family estate, known as Mount Adams, near Creswell. Margaret was the oldest of eleven children. William and Margaret married in 1834 in Baltimore and lived there until 1839, when they moved to Vicksburg, Mississippi, where William worked on a brickmaking venture that eventually failed, leaving them in serious financial difficulties. They moved back to the Webster farm in 1842. William then left with Margaret's brother, James, to search for gold in California. He returned three years later with a small amount of gold and purchased a farm from Theodore Gorrell; he then sold it eighteen months later, using the funds to purchase the Gover Hotel on Main Street from James Gover. Ironically, this was the first time William and Margaret found themselves in stable financial condition. In 1860, William and Margaret and their seven children resided, along with eleven other individuals, at the hotel on Main Street in Bel Air. Mr. Bissell advertised:

> *Having bought out the late proprietor of this well known establishment, I am prepared to accommodate my friends and the public generally, in a style equal to that of any hotel in the county. No expense will be spared to make guests comfortable, and my table will be supplied with all seasonable delicacies. The Bar will present an assortment of the best liquors; and nothing shall be left undone to make the house a first class Hotel.*

Everything seemed to be coming together at last, but Mr. Bissell grew increasingly concerned about the war and the need to "defend the rights of the South."

In January 1860, he joined the Harford Rifle Company, a local militia organized by William Dallam and Herman Stump Jr., whose sympathies were decidedly Southern. In 1861, with his wife two months pregnant with their eighth child, William Bissell left Bel Air to join the Eighth Virginia Infantry Regiment, part of Pickett's Division of the Confederate Army of Northern Virginia. He, like many others, believed that the war would be short and bloodless. Seven months later, the Bissells' eighth child, Mary Jarrett Bissell, was born.

In July 1863, Margaret received word that William was wounded at Gettysburg. He claimed that it was not serious, but she decided to try to reach him. She and her oldest daughter, Elizabeth, were able to make arrangements through relatives in the Union army to pose as members of the Christian Association who cared for the wounded. They took a coach to Magnolia Station and then a train to Baltimore, where they obtained passes to travel by train to Gettysburg. They were accompanied by three local Bel Air doctors—Richard Lee, Elin Hall Richardson and William Speed Richardson. The doctors helped them find lodging and assisted them throughout their ordeal. The trip took several days. Upon arriving in Gettysburg, they started their search for Mr. Bissell.

There were approximately twenty-one thousand wounded men, many lying in the muddy fields for days on end. Margaret finally found her husband at the Second Corps Hospital near Rock Creek, actually a series of tents that served as a hospital. He had been wounded numerous times, and the wounds were infected. Margaret asked the doctor in charge to allow her to nurse her husband and to put up a tent so he could have privacy. She dressed his wounds and made a bed and soup for him. Being a Confederate soldier, he would not normally have received the care of a personal surgeon and the nursing of his wife and daughter. William asked about his family and friends and cautioned his wife that none of the children should go to war—he was enough. He spoke of the many battles he had seen, but no matter how they tried, the infections kept worsening. Dr. Elin Hall Richardson decided that they had no choice but to amputate the arm. Mr. Bissell survived only a few hours after the operation. He died on July 17 and was buried near Gettysburg in a small Presbyterian churchyard. Bissell was one of only two Confederate soldiers granted burial in the churchyard with forty-eight Union soldiers. Margaret Bissell came back to Bel Air and died in 1906. Her daughter Elizabeth married Dr. Richardson soon after their return from Gettysburg.

THE BOOTH CONNECTION

The Bissells were not the only conflicted local family. Junius Booth, a pioneer of the American theater, raised his children just north of Bel Air at Tudor Hall. The home was designed as a country retreat for the family. Originally, the Booths lived in a log cabin on the property off Churchville Road. In 1847, Junius Booth built the Gothic Revival cottage that currently graces the property. The family experienced much tragedy here with the death of three of the Booth children. Edwin went on to achieve even greater fame and acclaim than his father. In 1850, at age seventeen, he and J.S. Clarke presented selections from several Shakespearean plays, sang and accompanied themselves on banjo and bones at the Harford County Courthouse. This was Booth's second appearance as a professional actor. From Bel Air, he went on to debut with the National Theater in New York in 1851. As his career progressed, he moved on to worldwide tours and eventually had his own theater in New York City. In his will, he left money to the town for use at the circulating library. However, since the library was no longer functioning, the funds were used to build a fountain in front of the courthouse in 1904.

His younger brother, John Wilkes, was never able to achieve the same level of importance in the theater but found notoriety in another way. At the end of the Civil War, passions ran strong among many of the former Southern sympathizers. While Edwin was very involved in the Union

Tudor Hall was the home of the Booth family. It is located just east of the town. *Courtesy of the Historical Society of Harford County.*

Edwin Booth was one of the most acclaimed Shakespearean actors of his day. Before leaving for the New York Theater, he appeared at the courthouse and other local venues.

John Wilkes Booth assassinated President Abraham Lincoln in April 1865.

cause and was a personal friend of the president, John harbored strong sympathies toward the Southern cause. He had unique access to the president because of his family's fame and was able to work with other Confederate sympathizers to conceive a plot to assassinate Lincoln at a performance at Ford's Theater in Washington, D.C. On April 14, 1865, John Wilkes Booth shot President Abraham Lincoln. The president never regained consciousness. The many accomplishments of the family were forever stained by this one heinous act. John Wilkes Booth was found hiding in a Virginia barn on April 24, 1865, and shot to death.

IV

A KINDER, SOMETIMES
GENTLER WORLD

POSTWAR BOOM

The pace of life in Bel Air and throughout the country increased after the Civil War. With the town's growth, local officials recognized a need to incorporate. Havre de Grace incorporated in 1785. By an act of the legislature, Bel Air became an incorporated town in 1874. Aberdeen followed in 1892, making it the third and last incorporated area in Harford County.

This was an era of wonder in many ways. The early, somewhat primitive houses gave way to massive Victorians. The railroad replaced the slow pace of horse and carriage travel; new industries sprang up around the railroad, and canning brought a newfound prosperity to area citizens, leading to leisure activities never before imagined.

Bel Air's town charter called for a charter commissioner form of government, with five commissioners elected every two years. The commissioners chose their own chairman. There was no mayor per se. Over time, this changed to four-year terms and a council manager form of government, but not until the 1970s. The town provided trash collection and road repair. It built streets and provided oversight of the new construction burgeoning throughout the town. Early legislation was minimal. For example, it covered regulations restricting pigs from wandering the streets and restrictions on new technology, such as the location and care of light poles.

One of the major factors in this new economy was the introduction of the canning industry. George T. Baker introduced modern canning technology to Harford County in the late 1860s, canning food in his farm kitchen in Aberdeen. Quickly, canning operations sprang up across the county. The canning houses needed and found a good water supply, either a stream or wells that could be relied on for a steady volume of water. They also needed a reasonably reliable transportation system. Local canneries shipped to Baltimore, Philadelphia and Wilmington using local rail connections. In the Bel Air area after 1883, this was the Maryland & Pennsylvania Railroad, known as the "Ma & Pa." A large labor pool was available among the immigrant population in Baltimore. Recently arrived immigrants from Poland and Bohemia came to the county from the city during the summer, living in one-room shanties with makeshift cooking areas. These were seasonal jobs processing tomatoes, corn and beans, but it provided necessary and steady work. Workers received chits based on their productivity. These could be used locally as cash. At the end of the season, these were exchanged for cash at the cannery.

Although the canneries were not actually in Bel Air, the town profited immensely as canning brokers, such as Robinson and Finney and Smith, Rouse and Webster, located around the courthouse; bankers provided financial services; attorneys provided legal services; warehouses clustered around the train station; and area retailers found a new market in meeting the needs of the numerous canneries. At one point, as many as 189 canneries existed in the county. A large portion of their product, supplies and labor force was dependent on the Ma & Pa Railroad, which ran through the northern quadrant of the town, and on the Bel Air brokers, who procured buyers for their products.

MARCH OF VICTORIANS

While this canning boom lasted, Bel Air's economy expanded. The courthouse remained the center of town activity, with new businesses and institutions surrounding it and fashionable residences sprouting up along Main Street, Bond Street and Broadway. Most of the new houses owed their design to architectural design manuals rather than professional architects. John Lingan, a local carpenter, built the Proctor

The Robinson Cassilly House is an example of one of the fine Victorian homes owned by prominent Bel Air families on Broadway. *Courtesy of the Town of Bel Air.*

House on Gordon Street, Saint Margaret's Chapel and the new one-room schoolhouse on Main Street. Jacob Bull, a local carpenter and self-trained architect, is credited with designing and building many of the Victorian-style homes along Broadway and Rockspring Avenue. Each of the houses kept its own unique flavor while following a basic Queen Anne style—two-and-a-half- to three-story design with wide porches, privet hedges and gracious tree-studded lawns. Many of the inns dating from this period project this same ambiance. In 1875, George Archer, a local resident and Princeton graduate who trained in Baltimore under George Frederick, opened an office in Bel Air. The town owes much of its present character to the buildings produced by George Archer and Jacob Bull between 1867 and 1900.

The houses reflected the best technology of the time with coal furnaces, iceboxes, gas fixtures and numerous outbuildings. In the early 1900s, the only way to preserve any large quantity of food was the icehouse. These were generally deep pits with A-line slate roofs, a door at one end and a ladder down to the bottom that were constructed in the backyards of the houses. Chunks of ice cut from a pond or river were put in and covered with straw for insulation. Food was wrapped carefully and kept there until needed. For those who didn't have the luxury of an icehouse or for larger storage needs, lockers were available on Ellendale Street in the town's industrial area. Town streets were busy from early morning until dusk, with coal delivery vehicles, ice wagons, milk trucks and hucksters singing out, "Strawberries, watermelons!"

Street life differed greatly from today as the lives of children and their parents centered primarily on the home and the day-to-day labor-intensive activities of homemaking, cooking and cleaning. Residents left a card in the window marking if they needed ice and how much. The iceman would then just come in the back door and fill the icebox. The coal wagons and later trucks worked in a similar manner, shoveling the coal into the coal bin. Neighborhoods were a beehive of activity with door-to-door salesmen, the milk and bread delivery wagons, hucksters and the like. In the spring, hoboes would ride the rails and come door-to-door looking to work for food. They had a permanent camp in the Heavenly Waters Valley, south of town, next to the railroad tracks. The gypsies also came every year in colorful clothes and decorated wagons. They camped north of town on Wysong's Meadow. They had a reputation for stealing, and nearly everyone was afraid of them. All children were warned to watch out for the gypsies because they stole children. Those who actually dared to visit the gypsy camp told a different story, praising the wonderful stew their hosts shared and the friendliness they experienced.

HORSE-AND-CARRIAGE DAYS

After the American Revolution, stagecoach service between Harford and Baltimore Counties became routine. The stage left the Dallam Hotel (earlier known as McIllhenny's) on Main Street in Bel Air, traveling via the turnpike, every Monday, Wednesday and Friday morning at 8:00 a.m. and reached Baltimore at 1:00 p.m. The stagecoach held fifteen passengers and suffered frequent breakdowns, robberies and accidents. These early coaches were essentially boxes on wheels. Over time, carriage manufacturers made some refinements to improve comfort, but road conditions made travel a test of endurance. Coaches often overturned or became mired in mud. Roads were generally clay or gravel, offering little in the way of comfort. Walking or driving in a horse and wagon were the most important means of transportation until the twentieth century introduced the automobile. Bel Air boasted many blacksmiths, wheelwrights, stables and carriage manufacturers available to meet the needs of area citizens. By the late 1800s, Bel Air had three carriage makers, four private livery stables and a harness and saddlers' shop, as well as a livery and stables at the various hotels. The dependence on horses and horse-drawn conveyances could be seen everywhere.

Enterprise Carriage Company, on Main Street at the site of the former Stagmer's Hotel, built carriages between 1893 and 1904. Earlier, James Colder and John Hanna, both on Main Street, also offered carriages, daytons, light and heavy farm wagons, blacksmithing and horseshoeing. Hanna also provided fine buggies and sleighs. An even larger operation, the Bullett Carriage Company, located on Thomas Street, opened in January 1889. Architect Jackson C. Gott designed the four-story frame building (42 by 198 feet), which Mr. Bullett and the Bel Air stockholders described as the "largest factory south of Wilmington." The company had a capacity to manufacture about three thousand vehicles annually. Fifty employees manufactured carriages, buggies and road carts in the fully mechanized operation. The first floor held a smith shop where workers hammered iron into various shapes for the buggies and a wood shop where cutting and smoothing various sides of the wagons took place. It also contained a showroom and an office. Workers cut the hickory, ash and poplar woods from Harford County and as far away as Indiana and Tennessee for use in constructing the carriages and wagons. The woods were rough cut on the second floor. The third floor contained the coloring and varnishing rooms, and the fourth floor was used for storage. Wheels and shafts came from the Hollingsworth Spoke Factory just outside town. Everything else was made on site. Orders came from Maryland, Pennsylvania and North Carolina. Business expanded quickly, and the enterprise became the major employer in Bel Air.

On September 19, 1891, Daniel Carroll, who lived in the residence across from the factory on Thomas Street, awoke to the cries of his child. Looking out his window, he saw flames shooting from the factory windows. He quickly rushed to warn the neighbors and generally raise the alarm. Neighbors pulled fifteen finished carriages from the burning building as firefighters dragged a hose from the jail on Main Street to the fire, a distance of about two blocks. Firefighters quickly realized the futility of efforts to save the factory and turned attention to protecting the four nearby dwellings. The heat from the fire was so intense that the legs

HUNDREDS OF VEHICLES

UNDER COURSE OF CONSTRUCTION AT THE FACTORY OF
THE

BULETT CARRIAGE CO.

A LARGE ASSORTMENT OF

FINISHED : WORK !

TO SELECT FROM.

We are now prepared to furnish the People of Harford and adjoining
Counties, *Fine and Durable Carriages of Various Styles and Grades;* at
prices much lower than such class of work has ever been offered for.

A visit to our Factory, where all the different styles and grades can be
seen under course of construction, will well repay the visitor for his trouble.

The Bullett Carriage Factory was the largest carriage manufacturer on the East Coast before it was destroyed by fire in 1891. *Courtesy of the Historical Society of Harford County.*

of a piano in a house near the fire blistered as the front door was opened. Wind swept coals from the fire toward the courthouse, forcing firefighters to wet down roofs in the vicinity to keep the fire from spreading further. To make matters worse, the reservoir for the town's water system, located three miles north of town, was not connected when the fire was discovered. Two firefighters, the Whitaker brothers, rushed by horse and buggy to the reservoir and had the water turned on in sixteen minutes.

Firefighters confirmed the fire starting point as the paint shop. The actual cause of the fire was never determined. Three people received serious injuries, and a nearby stable was also destroyed in the fire. The Bullett Factory had $47,000 in insurance, but the fire damage estimate was $90,000. Unfortunately, the company never recuperated from the loss. Auctioneers Matthews and Kirkland sold the company's remaining assets at the North Howard Street Repository on June 13, 1893. The loss to the town was enormous; many families lost their livelihoods and relocated, and the largest company in town disappeared.

BEL AIR AND THE MILKY WAY

In the 1870s, Bel Air still remained quite a small town. There were just a few streets, all lined with large trees, which met overhead and formed a lovely bower in the summer, even on Main Street. Over time, many of the trees disappeared, falling to power lines, Dutch elm disease, street widening and the like. Pressure grew to provide connections to Baltimore, Philadelphia and New York, resulting in the national road network and Route 1 through Bel Air's Main Street. This same concern encouraged local Bel Air businessmen to approach the Peach Bottom Railway executives to arrange for the new rail line from York, Pennsylvania, to extend into Harford County and down into Bel Air. The railroad did not have a charter to operate in the State of Maryland; thus began a long, arduous campaign to bring rail service to the county seat. Finally, in 1883, the City of Baltimore agreed to allow the Maryland Central Railroad to extend to Harford County through Bel Air if the county could provide the right of way and $120,000 toward the development of the line. A call went out to county citizens asking

> that every man on whose land the road may be located, shall be ready to give to our agent a relinquishment of the right of way and will add to this, such subscription as he may be able to make. To all others, whose land is not occupied by the road, we say, give us every dollar in subscription that you have or can borrow. In less than two years after the completion of the road it will be returned to you in the increased value of your property and business.

The first rails reached Bel Air from Baltimore in June 1883. A two-story station house soon followed with a waiting room, agent's telegraph office and controls for the Bel Air train order signal. The second floor was a residence for the railroad agent and his family. Additional land was available surrounding the station for extra tracks to be used as

The Ma & Pa Railroad station was a center of commercial and industrial growth from its beginnings in 1883 until its demise in 1959. *Courtesy of the Historical Society of Harford County.*

a yard, with a turning Y at the north end of the yard. Over time, the company changed hands and was renamed the Maryland and Pennsylvania in 1901. The railroad provided passenger, freight and mail service for the next seventy-one years. Yet even though it made at least thirty stops along its seventy-seven-mile line, it was a major boon to people working in Baltimore, schoolchildren, milk shippers, canners and farmers wanting to get their products to market. It was short, slow and not too dependable at times. Locals dubbed it the "Maybe & Perhaps/Misery & Patience."

Although slow and winding, the trip between Baltimore and Bel Air was picturesque and entertaining. Farmers could wave to the conductor to gain access to the train as it passed by. The local dairies shipped huge quantities of milk and dairy products to the city's waiting market, so much so that the Ma & Pa became known as the "Milky Way." The canneries shipped their products and brought in supplies daily. By 1949, twenty-eight different businesses were using the train to make bulk shipments out of Harford. Local citizens could shop at the big Baltimore department stores, spending a day at Hutzler's, Stewart's or the May Company, eating at the tearooms and restaurants that the stores hosted and return in the evening to await the stores' delivery wagons, which would bring the day's wonderful buys right to their doors.

By the mid-1950s, freight and passenger sales were declining as newly paved roads and the ever-expanding automotive and trucking industries created stiff competition for the line. Where residents once marveled at the scenic ride offered on the railroad, they now feared for their safety as the aging tracks and deteriorating trestles contributed to numerous accidents. All of these factors combined to force the railroad to start cutting services. Then the U.S. mail service notified the Ma & Pa that it would not renew its mail contract. The U.S. Postal Service shifted to trucking for the mail service. In 1959, the Ma & Pa discontinued all service from Baltimore to Whiteford. The last train headed north from Baltimore, and the rails were removed from the road bed and loaded on the train, ending Ma & Pa service except between Whiteford and York, Pennsylvania. Today, the Ma & Pa hiking trail follows the approximate line of the original rails, providing glimpses of the farms, streams and valleys that once depended so much on the train's services.

TECHNOLOGY BRINGS A NEW WAY OF LIFE

By 1890, technology had brought major changes to Bel Air and the rest of the country. Entrepreneurs began lobbying for public water systems, telephone service and gas and electric services. These new inventions, while embraced by a few, were frightening to many. Could this new technology be trusted? What were the costs? Would the expense be worthwhile in the long run?

J. Alexis Shriver embraced the technology fully, becoming one of the leading innovators in the community. He initiated the first local telephone company, operated from a small room in his home southwest of Bel Air. Eventually, he obtained a franchise, and by 1890, his company—the Baltimore and Bel Air Telephone Company—ran the first county telephone lines from Churchville to Bel Air. A switchboard at Hanway and Barnes Hardware Store handled all calls. This was on the northeast corner of Port Deposit Road (now Churchville Road) and Main Street. The switchboard later expanded and moved to Forwood's Drugstore.

The early telephones were clumsy wooden affairs that hung on the wall. The user cranked them to signal an operator. Usually, the phones were on two- or four-party lines, meaning four families shared a single line. To let you know a call was coming in, the operator connected to the party line on the switchboard. Each person on the party line had a different ring. For instance, you might have one long and two short rings for one party and two long rings for another so you had to listen closely. One of the challenges of the party system was the ability to listen in on all calls made to anyone on the party line. Privacy was not possible.

Locating the telephone poles needed for transmission proved quite difficult. Initially, the town board reacted by prohibiting pole construction altogether. Ordinance No. 10, adopted by the Bel Air Town Board in May 1879, prohibited obstruction of sidewalks, streets and gutters within the corporate limits by placement of telephone poles and wires by any individual or corporation. Several years later, the board reassessed its stand at the urging of Mr. Shriver and adopted regulations permitting poles and assessing a $1.50 tax on each pole. The Baltimore and Bel Air Telephone Company set about purchasing rights of way from individual property owners so that pole construction could begin. Having a local telephone system provided many conveniences but also some challenges if residents wanted to call someone outside Bel Air. In 1921, the Chesapeake and Potomac Telephone Company (C&P) and the Baltimore and Bel Air Telephone Company reached an agreement to consolidate. Mr. Shriver became C&P's local representative, with an office on Courtland Street and Dallam Place (now Hickory Avenue), and service became more unified.

The town initially contracted with the Reckord Manufacturing Company in 1894 to supply the town lighting using its steam generator. Eventually, Reckord Manufacturing updated its generating plant on Winters Run and sold the plant to the Bel Air Electric Company in 1902. J. Alexis Shriver served on the board of this company as well. By 1905, electricity was beginning to be available throughout town, although not yet in the surrounding countryside. Numerous providers vied for customers. In 1928, the Consolidated Gas and Electric, Light and Power Company of Baltimore became the primary provider (later known as Baltimore Gas & Electric or BGE) with a gas plant located on Pennsylvania Avenue. The Bel Air Electric Company built a hydroelectric plant on Winters Run at Pat Howard's Mill south of Bel Air and downstream

This dam was built on Winters Run to generate electricity for the Bel Air Electric Company. *Courtesy of the Historical Society of Harford County.*

from Baltimore Pike. The turbine generators provided electricity for the general neighborhood. The plant included a holding pond at Lake Fanny, as well as ice for local icehouses and an ice-skating rink for area residents. Earlier, steam power technology, and now the introduction of electricity, had brought major changes to the entire community. Some businesses disappeared altogether; others faced major adjustments, as did the residents. The quiet, simple life of earlier times was fast disappearing.

In addition to these new innovations, pressure began to build to take advantage of new technologies available to provide a more reliable and safe water system for the town. In 1890, the town board adopted an ordinance establishing a fee to be paid to Bel Air Water and Light, another of Mr. Shriver's companies, for water mains of a specific size and length together with fire plugs suitable and sufficient for fire extinguishing, street sprinkling and domestic water service purposes. The ordinance also provided for construction of a reservoir capable of holding one million gallons of water and situated at an elevation not less than ninety feet above the surface of the roadway in front of the courthouse, and construction of an eight-inch pipe to be laid along Main Street from Rockspring Road to Baltimore Pike. The company built a reservoir, three miles north of town, near the intersection of what are now Maryland Routes 23 and 24. The reservoir may have saved the town the next year as the night's winds swept embers toward Main Street from the catastrophic fire at the Bullett Carriage Company.

Eventually, American Water Works purchased the Bel Air Water and Light Company, along with water systems in Westminster, Ellicott City and Willoughby Beach. Over time, the system upgraded to include two additional water towers, numerous new lines and a deep well near Bynum Run. The company changed hands over the years, but the private water system is still in effect in the Bel Air area.

The most long-lasting and dramatic changes came with the introduction of the automobile and the new roads needed for the cars, trucks and buses that became the primary source of transportation. The horse and buggy quickly faded from the local scene, as did the local blacksmiths, wheelwrights and carriage shops; even the horses' drinking fountain, provided by Edwin Booth in front of the courthouse, was moved to the front lawn area to make way for parking along Main Street.

At this time, the state legislature established an act to incorporate a turnpike company, which then raised funds to construct a crushed stone roadway in the area designated by the act. This was a labor-intensive and cumbersome method of providing hard surface roads. With the development of a macadam road construction process, building hard surface roads became much simpler but still quite expensive. An English builder named McAdam developed the process of binding broken stone and stone dust under pressure and using a quantity of water to seal the mass together in 1836, but it was not until 1898 that Bel Air got its first macadam road. William Woolsey, a Churchville farmer, left a trust to his two sisters, and at their deaths the remaining funds were to be used to construct "macadamized" roads in Harford County. Mr. Woolsey's will specified five roads but noted that the first should be a road from Churchville to Bel Air. The others were to follow based on the adequacy of the remaining funds. The trust fund amounted to $60,000 by 1898, which allowed construction of only one macadam road, Churchville Road leading to Bel Air.

With the growing pressure to improve county roads, the county commissioners reluctantly accepted the responsibility for planning, designing and constructing new roads rather than depending on private roads and the old turnpike system. The state also felt the pressure to upgrade its road system. By 1910, the State Roads Commission had completed a hard surface road between Bel Air and Conowingo. Newspaper reports of the day noted that "the values of the property situated on each side of these roads is greatly increased." The road was completed as far as Kalmia in the fall and reached Forge Hill in the summer, changing the route to follow along the edge of the ridge, resulting in the building of a new bridge over Deer Creek and eliminating the long and tedious grades on both sides of the stream. The work was very trying. Rock in the area made it necessary to revert from the steam shovel to pick and mattock. A *Sun* reporter noted, "When this piece of work is completed, two and a half miles of the most disagreeable highway to travel in Harford County will be done away with".

Former blacksmiths, liveries and carriage shops now looked to the future, transforming into service stations, garages and car dealers. MacLean's livery on Courtland Street became MacLean's Garage, advertising expert work, prompt service and its new role as a Ford agency. The hardware store on the corner of Courtland and Main Streets became an Essex

An early example of the "autobus" service provided by the McMahon Bus Company from Bel Air to and from Baltimore.

dealer with a sample car in the front window. The Hanna Carriage Company was now a car dealer. Trucks became equally popular, meeting the needs of local farmers, and bus services appeared throughout the county. Harry Hopkins provided a bus between Aberdeen and Havre de Grace, and another server operated buses between Baltimore and Darlington. The McMahon Bus Company was the longest-lasting bus service, providing direct access from Bel Air to Baltimore daily. Local businesses featured ads touting the bus service. In one example, Kisling's Drugstore posted this advertisement:

It is just an hour and a half ride by auto from Baltimore City to Bel Air, Md, that pretty town located in the beautiful hills of Harford County. Bel Air is the county seat of Harford County with a population of over 1,500.

It is on the new national Lincoln Highway about half-way between Baltimore and Havre de Grace, Md. It is on the direct route from Washington, D.C., to Philadelphia, Atlantic City and New York City. All roads that lead to Bel Air are good roads—they are as smooth as a billiard ball. You cannot select a more interesting or beautiful ride than the one to Bel Air and nearby country. Regular meals can be had at the Kenmore Inn, Grangers' Hotel and the Country Club Inn. Light lunches such as chicken, tongue, ham and cheese sandwiches with coffee or milk, also pies and cakes, can be had at the Korner Konfectionery at any time.

The soda Garden at Kisling's is just the place to stop for a cooling glass of soda or a sundae. It is located at Kisling's (BelAir's Best Drug Store) on Main Street, opposite the Post office. Look for the Big Electric Sign and the name—Kisling's. The Garden was built and opened last June and all during the summer we had from two to four autobus parties from Baltimore each week and many smaller auto parties from everywhere. Why not get up an autobus party and motor to Bel Air and stop at the Garden? The Garden is right out in the open air, made of lattice, covered with running vines and sweet scented blossoms. The tables, chairs and other furnishing are of a rustic effect. The cooling breezes are always present, making the Garden very inviting indeed. [Victrola music.] In this Garden you will be served with the famous Kisling sodas and sundaes.

Pleasure clubs find an autobus party a reasonable and pleasant evening's outing. Buses and cars can be had from McMahon Bros. Co.

of Overlea and Bel Air and Marx Bros. of Overlea. You can get on Bel Air Road electric cars and ride to Overlea and have the bus meet you or you can have the bus call for you in the city at your clubhouse.

The idea of bringing customers and tourists to Bel Air was very popular at this time. An April 1905 news article boasts a newly formed auto club, fashioned similar to examples in Europe. The club promoted touring and sightseeing in the Bel Air–Carney corridor. The trip included the homes of the late Edwin Booth, ex-governor William Paca, a signer of the Declaration of Independence, the Susquehanna Bridge, a slate quarry, Deer Creek and the scenery along the Susquehanna and other points of interest. This was a joint venture with the Bel Air Electric Company, whose officers were J. Alexis Shriver, John D. Worthington, George Van Bibber, E.O. Kirkland, Charles Bonaparte, J.S. Griffith and Albert Gordon. They saw a chance of shaping the destiny of both their company and the fledgling electric railway, which would travel through "some of the most beautiful scenery in Maryland."

The electric railway never caught on, and the auto clubs flourished through the 1920s and then disappeared, but the roadways continued to improve, and people continued to discover Bel Air and Harford County. George Van Bibber, a Bel Air artist and writer, describes wandering through the parking lot behind the Kenmore Inn on Sunday afternoons as a child between 1910 and the 1920s. The cars on the lot included all the prestigious vehicles of the day—Pierce Arrows; limousines; long, low Loziers and Wintons—many with gas headlights and brilliantly polished brass and chrome. The motoring clubs frequented the Kenmore Inn as an assembly place, meeting in the grand dining hall. Guests included the Vanderbilts, Biddles and Drexels.

BUSINESS AND INDUSTRY

The automobile age brought fumes, dust, noise and traffic. It also brought easy access and opened up new business opportunities for the county. Felix Irwin came to Bel Air from North Carolina in 1921 and purchased the 220-acre Holland farm at Del Haven on Route 1 (Moores Mill Road and Conowingo Road). With U.S. Route 1 passing by the farm and no

The Irwin family built the hotel and cabins on part of their farm along U.S. Route 1 to serve the motoring public. This was one of the first such facilities in Maryland, foreshadowing today's motel industry. *Courtesy of the Town of Bel Air.*

places for tourists to stay overnight, people began informally camping on the property. Mrs. Irwin recognized a potential business opportunity and started to rent space for travelers to camp on the corner of their farm overnight. This soon became a popular stopping point for interstate travelers, leading to the development of thirteen tourist cabins, a twelve-room motel with four baths and a kitchen, a restaurant with two dining rooms and a roof garden, as well as a swimming pool that served the community well for many years. Mr. and Mrs. Irwin developed the first motel business in the county, doing so well that they expanded with another motel operation in College Park, Maryland.

Farming remained the primary pursuit for most of the county's citizens well into the twentieth century. The area around Bel Air was blessed with fertile soil, gentle hills and abundant water supply from nearby streams. Over time, word spread to the hills of North Carolina and western Virginia that farmland was available, and many farmers, hard hit by the Depression, the depletion of the forests in Appalachia and the local primogenitor tradition—whereby the farm went to the oldest son, leaving the others to fend for themselves—decided to relocate to Harford County, many in the Bel Air area. This migration pattern, along with the tremendous technological advances of the era, changed the social, economic and political future of the community. The new residents brought a strong work ethic, along with many traditions new to the community.

In the early 1900s, James Newkirk of Floyd County, Virginia, came to Harford County and returned to visit relatives in Ashe County, North Carolina, with such glowing reports that others soon followed him. Wiley Winton Osborne, a leading citizen of Ashe County, decided to see for himself, having recently sold his land to settle his first wife's estate. He found good farmland in the Thomas Run Valley and moved there in 1913 with his son Muncie and son-in-law, Grover C. Greer. Other sons and brothers and sisters of the Greers soon followed. These new residents cited that the end of the dairying program and the wreck of the cheese-making plans by Mr. Farnham in the North Carolina Extension service resulted in the loss of a number of good citizens. A large group of Ashe County's best citizens disposed of their farms and moved to Bel Air. Among them were W.C., Ed, Clive and John Greer, John and Charley Jones, Wilburn Thompson, Robert Livesey and Columbus Young. In fact, there were so many of them that the area around Bel Air became known as the Ashe County community for many years. For a time, there were so many emigrants from these areas that the *Jefferson Skyland Post* was regularly running ads reading, "Edwards Bus leaves on such and such a date for Bel Air, MD."

The Irwins were among these North Carolina transplants; another was Orley G. Reedy. Born in 1883 in Troutdale, North Carolina, he bought the Majors Choice farm just east of Hickory Avenue (Route 1) from the Lawrence McCormick family in 1929. The farm was part of a 600-acre land grant from the British Crown dating back to early colonial times. It contained an eleven-room stone house with several fireplaces and many outbuildings. By the time Mr. Reedy and his wife and seven children purchased the property, it consisted of 133 acres. Under Mr. Reedy's management, the farm was one of the most productive farms in the county, producing chickens, turkeys, cows and hogs. Mr. Reedy shipped the farm's products to Baltimore on the Ma & Pa train and by truck.

The town at the time was still quite small and reeling from the national economic troubles. There were a few inns, three banks, two drugstores and a dry goods store (Harbor and Price). The Depression

The Majors Choice land grant dates back to the 1700s. This is the original farmhouse that now sits in the center of a modern housing development. *Courtesy of the Historical Society of Harford County.*

had a sharp impact on the farm community, but the banks were even more severely hit. Two of the three banks closed within a few years of Mr. Reedy's move. Second National Bank paid depositors 65 percent on their accounts before closing, trying to make things right with its customers. Later, the bank vice-president took his own life in despair over the bank's failure. In many instances, depositors lost all of their savings. The Reedys farmed the land until 1984. It was then sold to a developer. Today, although the house remains, the rest of the farm is gone and replaced by more than four hundred homes and two small parks at the northern boundary of the town.

Many more families followed, some as farmers and later many as workers in various trades throughout the county. This group of migrants, often called "Down Yonders," went on to become a major influence in the county politically, economically and culturally.

While the courthouse formed the center of town, gathering businesses and institutions around it, the north side of town became the catalyst for industrial development. In stark contrast to today, the railroad, the central location and the prestige of a county seat designation were very important for industries. As soon as the railroad announced its intention to build in Bel Air, existing and new businesses began expanding around the station site. The land owned by a few local families quickly changed hands to become a significant part of the community's economy. The area next to the railroad line was ideally located near farms, residences and businesses. It had ready access to the railroad and county road network. It was convenient for area citizens and visitors. The businesses were owned by a few local families and some larger corporations. Many of these early families are still in the area. The Reckord Mill is now operated by the Holloway family, not the Reckords. It still provides service to area farmers, although these services changed dramatically in recent years. The Corbin family, who started the Corbin Coal and Ice Company, transformed it into the Corbin Fuel Oil Company. Each of these family-owned businesses grew and prospered in the area by meeting the changing needs of area residents. They became part of a closely linked network of businesses that surrounded the Ma & Pa station, forming a small industrial complex.

The mill met the farmers' needs for grain processing and supplies. The train went directly through the mill complex, providing easy access to markets to the north and south. Dairy farmers brought milk cans to the Ma & Pa warehouse directly across from the station for distribution to the city markets. Corbin provided a storage facility in the days before refrigeration was readily available to individuals. It provided door-to-door ice and coal delivery to homes throughout the county. As times changed, the company restructured to provide oil storage and services. With the increasing demand for oil, the American Oil Company developed an oil tank facility and service station, providing oil and gas to area dealers. Its facilities next to the railroad warehouse helped form a major oil distribution center. The McComas family operated a large lumberyard and hardware store on either side of North Main Street just south of the train station and the mill. Unlike today's industrial complexes, this was an area bustling with people using the train station, storing materials, picking up supplies and sharing a camaraderie scarce in today's communities. The Aberdeen Concrete Company, situated behind the hardware store, helped supplement the lumberyard's and hardware store's products. Meats and groceries could be purchased at Roy Coale's Meat Market next to the lumberyard. A small hotel provided accommodations near the hardware store. Homes, churches and farmland could be found within a block of the industrial complex. In the summer, area children would follow the ice trucks in the hope of getting the drivers' attention and a treasured piece of ice. The train would stop all traffic on Main Street, and pedestrians would simply walk through the train to the other side or sit and wait, knowing this was an inevitable part of the day. Local hotels provided shuttle service between the hotels and the station on a regular basis, creating a constant buzz of activity.

South of the train station, new businesses grew to meet the modernizing town. Grocery stores, shops and restaurants appeared offering services and products never before seen in the county. Hotels and boardinghouses expanded to meet the increasing population. National chains, such as the Atlantic & Pacific Tea Company and Acme Food stores, located on Main Street. Family businesses such as Hirsch's Men's Store, Getz Clothing Store and Coppel's shoe store opened on Main Street. Mr. and Mrs. Solomon Getz moved to Bel Air from Duncannon, Pennsylvania, in 1895. At first, they rented a building on Main Street for a clothing store. Over time, they were able to buy 26 South Main Street, living above the store with their children. The Getz children went on to become doctors, lawyers and jewelers. The clothing store is now a legal office. The jewelry store that once inhabited a small section of the clothing store is now in Harford Mall.

Hirsch's Men's Store opened in 1924. Benjamin Hirsch came from Philadelphia and located his tailoring and haberdashery shop on Main Street and Lee Street. In 1926, he moved to 9 South Main Street. The business served Harford County residents until 2009, when Mr. Hirsch's son-in-law, David Cohen, turned ninety and decided that it was time to retire. The entire community felt the loss of this treasured landmark and trusted friend. Similarly, the Coppels came to Bel Air with their family in 1926 from Baltimore City. Mr. Coppel, a shoemaker, opened a store just north of Pennsylvania Avenue on North Main Street. Mr. and Mrs. Coppel lived above the store with their three children until the 1940s, when the family moved back to Baltimore. Next to Hirsch's, Harry Schleider operated the Bel Air 5¢-$1 Department Store. The property owners required that Mr. Schleider arrange and pay for all coal delivery and removal of ashes. At this time, most of the stores and homes in Bel Air had coal furnaces. Generally, this meant shoveling the coal ash from the basement coal bin area and spreading the ash in the adjoining alley.

Prior to Mr. Schleider, the site was the home of the Harford Garage (in the rear) and Crook's store in the front portion of the building. Eventually, Schleider's store became part of the Woolworth chain.

This was the era of first-floor businesses, with the owners' residences located above the stores. This arrangement ensured constant activity along the street and provided a sense of community. Main Street and Bond Street hosted numerous general stores, markets, dressmakers, tailors, bakers and wine and liquor merchants. Dean & Foster Funeral Parlor provided dual service as a cabinetmaker and undertaker. Nathan Dean started the business in 1900. Joseph Foster came in as a partner several years later, after Mr. Dean's sons took over the business.

In 1858, a town directory identifying local businesses and professions listed twenty-seven attorneys, five doctors and one dentist. The legal profession was by far the most prominent in Bel Air. Attorneys provided many of the services that we associate with other types of institutions today, e.g. banks, realtors and mortgage brokers. There was no such thing as a mortgage as we perceive it today. To buy a house, an individual paid cash or worked with an attorney, who would find someone willing to loan money for a certain term. Particularly after the Civil War, many widows placed funds with an attorney, who arranged loans to bring in interest on the funds. In 1863, the Federal government first authorized national banks, but even then Harford County did not charter a bank until 1881. Before that time, anyone wishing to invest or borrow money at a banking institution had to travel to Baltimore or Annapolis. The first bank in Bel Air was organized in 1881 as Harford National Bank with a capital stock of $50,000. It located on Wall Street between the Masonic Temple and the courthouse. Mary Hall tells of her father, who was vice-president of the Harford Bank, driving to Aberdeen Proving Grounds and Edgewood Arsenal twice a week to provide bank services, his only protection his .38 revolver. The army post brought a lot of extra money into the county, and those bank trips were probably the forerunner of branch banks.

With the Crash of '29, the banks and the county's fortunes changed dramatically. The bank operated until 1933. In 1888, the Second National Bank opened on Office Street, again failing in 1933, like so many others during the Great Depression. Two more banks followed. In 1900, Commercial and Savings Bank opened, initially in a small rented room in the Masonic Temple and later on Main Street. The bank was demolished in 2012 to make way for a town parking lot. The other bank, Farmers and Merchants Bank, opened in 1909. In 1933, President Roosevelt ordered all banks in the nation to close to address the concerns of the national economy. Once the closing order was lifted, three of Bel Air's banks—Harford National, Farmers and Merchants and Second National—consolidated to form First National Bank of Bel Air. The new bank located on Office Street in the old Second National Bank building. W. Wylie Hopkins became its first president and served until his death in 1938.

The one county financial institution that was available to residents before the Civil War was Harford Mutual Insurance Company, formed in 1842 to provide fire insurance. The company was based on the model of the London companies organized in the 1600s. An applicant gave a note of hand, which would bear 6 percent and was subject to call anytime there was a loss. Originally located at 33 West Courtland Street, the company traded the building to a canning broker, Smith/Webster, in 1921 and moved to 18 Office Street. At that time, the building was frame and relatively small. By 1929, Harford Mutual had outgrown its space and contracted with John Hamme, a Pennsylvania architect, to design and build a new brick structure on the site. The building is now owned by Harford County. The insurance company moved to new, larger headquarters on North Main Street in 1963 and remains one of the town's largest employers.

One of the more interesting businesses to locate in Bel Air in the early 1900s was the Fulford Hickman Company, built to bottle carbonated beverages and soft drinks. There were three partners: Alexander Fulford; his brother, Frank; and a friend, Claude Hickman, with $25,000 in capital to begin the venture. Initially, the company, located at the corner of Main Street and Fulford Lane (now Avenue) did well, issuing 814 shares at $10 each in January 1917. They operated the business from a small stone building behind the main house, which housed vats on the second floor, filling bottles below. On the west side of the building was a huge glass-lined water distillation plant over a coal fire. Distilled water went by pipe into a filling and capping machine. On the east side of the plant was a garage storing an old white truck used to deliver cases of bottles to various stores. The company made Lord Calvert Ginger Ale, birch beer, sarsaparilla, cream soda and strawberry soda. Coca-Cola, which was a fledgling company at the time, offered it a franchise for bottling Coca-Cola, but the company turned it down, thinking that Coke would never catch on.

Fulford Hickman Company operated from this small building, processing soft drinks such as root beer, sarsaparilla and lemon soda. *Courtesy of the Town of Bel Air.*

Alex Fulford was a veteran of the Spanish-American War and was called up to serve when war was declared (World War I) in 1918. This proved disastrous for the company. Equity dockets show that the lender foreclosed on the company's loans because Mr. Fulford was "not taking care of his business" due to his military duty. He was serving in France at the time. The property was sold at auction. In time, the Loyola Federal Bank purchased the property and demolished the house for a new bank. It is now owned by SunTrust Bank. The small stone building served many purposes over the years and is now a candy store.

HOTELS, INNS AND TAVERNS

Hotels, inns and taverns were integral parts of town life from its very beginnings. The Union Tavern, owned by Thomas Hays, whose wife inherited it from her father in the early 1800s, was on the northwest corner of Main Street and Baltimore Pike. This was a major gathering place for local politicians for many years. After a series of owners and several name changes, it was demolished in the 1960s to make way for the Equitable Trust Bank building. Similarly, most of the local inns had several lives as owners changed and times demanded new approaches to business.

The earliest and one of the most interesting hotels was the Eagle Hotel. In 1718, C.B. Todd built this inn on what is now Bond Street across from the courthouse. At the time, there was little else in the area and certainly no thought of Bel Air being the county seat or the home of the county courthouse. The weatherboard-covered log building contained a massive fireplace, long porches and twelve-inch log beams. Originally, it served travelers and the few local settlers in the area. Over time, it became a meeting place for politicians, businessmen and those attending sessions of the court. Major William Richardson, a veteran of the War of 1812, purchased the fifty-two-acre parcel from Buckler and Joshua Bond in 1821. Major Richardson and his wife operated under the name Richardson's Tavern. In the 1830s, the front approach to the inn was guarded by a cannon reportedly from the Battle of Brandywine. Mrs. Richardson took over operation of the hotel after her husband's death

Richardson's Drugstore, built by Dr. William Richardson, served Bel Air for many years. Its soda fountain enhanced the pharmacy and served as a popular local gathering place for downtown workers and area students. It is now used as physicians' offices. *Courtesy of the Historical Society of Harford County.*

in 1843 and changed the name to Mrs. Richardson's Hotel, hoping to modify the rowdy image then associated with taverns. The Richardsons had three sons: Henry, who became a county sheriff and later a farmer; Dr. William Richardson, the owner of Richardson's Pharmacy and for a time the register of wills; and Dr. E. Hall Richardson, who in addition to his medical practice went on to become a major developer in town and the owner of a large home, known as Indian Hill, on North Main Street that would later become the Yew Tree Inn. Samuel McGraw took over the Eagle Hotel between 1858 and the mid-1870s. Around 1916–17, Howard S. O'Neill and some of his associates decided to organize the hotel premises into a country club, changing the name and adding some amenities. They immediately constructed clay tennis courts next to the hotel, but World War I intervened, and plans never progressed beyond that point. However, the name stuck, and the community continued to enjoy the enchantment of the rambling inn with its flowing porches, massive trees and gardens. The fireplace in the lounge boasted a gigantic pair of andirons, each crowned by a shining brass ball almost a foot in diameter. The lounge itself was a graciously furnished room two stories high with a second-floor gallery fronted by a delicate railing of simple elegance. The upper story included a bronze vine with translucent glass flowers that glowed with an exotic brilliance when the lights came on.

The Yew Tree Inn property is now the home of the Harford Mutual Insurance Company. *Courtesy of the Historical Society of Harford County.*

Once home to Bel Air's elite, the Country Club Inn was demolished to make way for Bel Air's first shopping center.

This was the center of society for Bel Air's elite. People rented the lounge for "invitation dances," hiring a band and enjoying an evening of dance and music. The hotel continued into the 1940s under the ownership of Mr. and Mrs. Herbert Hanna, but the surrounding property was sold off in separate parcels over the years. Each operator expanded and enhanced the inn until it grew into a rambling U-shaped building of two stories with cooling shade trees and deep verandas around it and an occasional dormer breaking the gable roofline. The inn was eventually abandoned in the 1940s and rented for a time to Russell and Kate Lord, who published the national magazine *The Land* from there, as well as lived in the rambling old building. Russell Lord described the inn as follows:

> *In summers the abandoned inn was a mushroom cellar as to dampness and in winter an old fashioned icebox as to chill. The lease which governed our time of abode in the Inn should be framed and preserved as an historic document signifying wartime contingencies under unusually spacious conditions…And yet, the Landmark was a seemly place in which to dwell for a while before it crumbled. Built in 1718, it remained serenely inhabited by companionable spirits. The game room*

was a good place for an office, if there is any good place for that. The front room, once the taproom, with the name of G. Washington carved with a diamond on a windowpane (an amiable forgery in all likelihood) was flanked with high galleries and two fireplaces, which still drew. You could give a party for sixty in that great room. Its original elegance had somewhat faded. It looked its best in the evening under low lamplight; but it remained the living heart of a gracious habitation to the end. A shiny chain store with a paved parking lot is destined to mark the spot any week now. This is called progress.

The Gover Hotel, on the southeast corner of Main and Courtland Streets, was initially operated by Stephen Jones in 1814 but owned by the Hays-Jacob family. Around 1830, James Gover took over management of the hotel and expanded it to include a two-story front porch. In 1857, William Bissell acquired the hotel and lived there with his wife and children until the Civil War. His wife continued operating the hotel after William's death at Gettysburg. The next owner of record revised the name to the Granger Hotel in 1878. It had dining rooms, a lobby and a taproom on the first floor, with rooms above. According to one account in *Bel Air: The Town through Its Buildings*:

[T]*hese were not private rooms nor could they be reserved: one took pot-luck as to roommates in those days. All gentlemen were requested to remove their boots before retiring. Ladies could always have a private room, delicacy being natural to the weaker sex. If the rooms upstairs were full, even to the dormers in the attic, a traveler might curl up before the fire in the taproom and sleep there until he was turned out by the early breakfast trade.*

In 1918, John Hopkins, the owner at that time, sold the property to F. Bond Boarman and his brother-in-law, William W. Bradford, for use as a hardware store. Boarman and Bradford started their business at Churchville Road and Main Street in 1910, when they purchased David Hanway's hardware store. They sold everything from horse blankets to stoves, furnaces and automobile supplies. Within a few years, they outgrew the space and purchased the hotel, which was within a block of their original store but provided more room and opportunity. The new owners completely renovated the building and expanded the hardware store line to include Hudson and Essex automobiles, one of which was showcased in the front window of the store. The store advertised regularly, citing "the Hudson Super-Six excellence in art and engineering. Whether it is the Woman of good taste and distinction or the man who must have flexibility, power, constant dependability—the wish is gratified in the Super-Six cars."

At the time, there were no service stations per se. Bel Air's Main Street, as a major route between Baltimore and Philadelphia, was heavily traveled. Boarman & Bradford seized the opportunity to provide gas and oil from a tank located at the curb on Main Street. The store continued to sell hardware store staples, farm supplies, stoves and furnaces but also sold tires and automobile accessories. In 1920, William Bradford left the firm. Then tragedy struck in 1923, when Mr. Boarman suffered a heart attack at a dance at the Harford Boat Club. He was in the middle of a dance and simply asked his partner to stop dancing, collapsed to the floor and died. He was only forty-six years of

Serving area citizens since the early 1800s as Gover's Hotel, then Granger's Hotel and eventually becoming Courtland Hardware store, this building was demolished to make way for a new office building in the 1980s. *Courtesy of the Historical Society of Harford County.*

age. The store went to his sister, Bessye, who managed it until 1952, when her nephew Horace Boarman took over and changed the name to Courtland Hardware. Gene Graybeal soon became his partner, and together they took the business to new heights. In 1979, Jim Kunkel and Richard Thomas purchased the store when Mr. Graybeal decided to retire. They operated from this location until the mid-1980s, but growing demand for space and parking led them to seek a new location on Bond Street. The new owners demolished the old hotel and replaced it with an office building. Courtland Hardware is still in town, but now on Bond Street, still featuring hardware items and stoves as it continues to serve the town and county residents.

Ms. Sarah Forwood and her mother managed Granger's Hotel at the time of the hotel's sale to Bradford and Boarman. Hoping to continue in the hotel business, they purchased a building for a new hotel/boardinghouse at the northeast corner of Gordon and Main Streets. They named the new venture the Circle Inn, which quickly became a favorite boardinghouse location for local teachers. The Yew Tree Inn across the street from the Circle Inn also offered a convenient location near the train station. Originally the family home of Dr. E. Hall and Alice Bissell Richardson (daughter of William and Margaret Bissell), the property was known as Indian Hill. The rambling Victorian house became the home of the Rouse family for a time and then was sold in the 1930s to the owners of the Yew Tree Inn. The hotel was named for the large yew tree in the front yard. This proved to be an ideal setting for an inn, with its expansive drive and pastoral surroundings. In 1963, Harford Mutual Insurance moved its offices to the site of the former inn, building a new office facility to meet its growing needs.

With the Country Club Inn, Granger's Hotel, Stagmer's Hotel (situated on the southwest corner of Main Street and Courtland Street) and Dunnigan's Hotel (on the southeast corner of Bond Street and Courtland Street), local hotels encircled the courthouse, providing food, lodging and drink. Stagmer's and the Dallam Hotel, located next to the jail, worked together in the early days. Mrs. Dallam sold coach tickets for travelers going to Edgewood to catch a train to Baltimore or Philadelphia. (Before the Ma & Pa came to Bel Air, this was one of the few options available.) Travelers would then go to Stagmer's Hotel to board the coach. The Dallam Hotel later became the Vaughn Hotel and served well into the twentieth century.

The Dallam Hotel eventually became the Vaughn Hotel and a prominent part of Main Street life.

Barbara Ferry, a widow with several children, built Dunnigan's Hotel on Courtland Street in 1868–69. The next year, she married Bernard Dunnigan, bailiff of Judge Watter's court. Mr. Dunnigan opened a tavern with a liquor store in the basement of the hotel, which operated until local option arrived. Mr. Dunnigan ran the liquor store/tavern, while Mrs. Dunnigan took care of the hotel. The tavern proved to be very popular.

The local option law went into effect on May 1, 1893, causing a riot to break out in Bel Air on Monday night when a large number of people gathered in town, several thinking it was their last chance to get a legal drink. Many indulged too freely. As the night grew later, the group became noisy and quarrelsome. Mrs. Forwood, recognizing the trouble ahead, closed Granger's Hotel. Dunnigan's, however, stayed open. About 11:00 p.m., a number of young men at the liquor store started a general mêlée. By the time it was over, one man was shot and several others were injured.

The Kenmore Inn came somewhat later when Colonel Harry Hanway purchased the old Munnikhuysen house and office at the corner of Main

Dunnigan's served as one of the Courthouse Square meeting places, offering rooms, food and drink. The tavern entrance was on the side in the lower level along Bond Street. *Courtesy of the Town of Bel Air.*

The Kenmore Inn focused on meeting the needs of the automobile age and the newly formed motoring clubs of the 1910–20 era. *Courtesy of the Historical Society of Harford County.*

Street and Baltimore Pike from Captain Richard Bouldin in 1894. He then built a Second Empire–style hotel and dining room that became a popular gathering place in Bel Air. Year by year, Colonel Hanway added dining rooms and new floors of rooms. While this was occurring, he made arrangements for demolition of the old row houses across the street, making the hotel much more visible. He added a parking lot toward Baltimore Pike screened by a geometrically trimmed hedge and surrounded by a wide sidewalk. A wide walkway led across the level green lawn, shaded by magnificent old maples, ash trees and oaks. The northern end of the lawn was cut by a driveway curving in from the intersection of Main Street and Baltimore Pike. The entire sand-colored pebble lot stretched westward downhill to the hotel's garage and utility buildings. The true purpose of the hotel—to serve the various motoring clubs in those days—soon became apparent. Driving at the time was still an adventure—never knowing when a tire would blow out or the road map would lead one astray. Therefore, having a place to eat and spend the night was crucial. The hotel flourished until the 1960s, when it, like so many of the other large hotels, was demolished to make way for yet another supermarket. By the 1970s, all of Bel Air's hotels and inns were gone, victims of the automobile age and the changing lifestyles of the twentieth century.

Schools and Institutions

The expansion of the local school system, the development of new churches, the beginning of a library system and the development of the town's first police and fire departments followed the conclusion of the Civil War. Before the war, most schools were private facilities, making education something generally reserved for the well-to-do. In 1695, the General Assembly passed legislation taxing "skin exports" for support of free schools, but a letter from the governor of the province tells of the sparseness of settlement and the distance between homesteads and offers the opinion that people were not interested in the common school methods of education. In 1812, certain funds were set aside by the Maryland legislature to assist in schooling the children of parents too poor to pay tuition, and in 1826 the legislature passed an act providing for the establishment of public schools throughout the state. Unfortunately, none of these actions resulted in the development of any large number of public schools. Finally, in 1864, the state appointed a state Board of Education and accompanying local boards, with members to be named by the judge of the circuit court. This spurred school development.

Still, from 1867, when the state constitution required development of a local school system, until 1920, most county schools were one- or two-room affairs. Private schools like the Bel Air Academy continued to provide their services to many of the town's leading citizens and received subsidies from the state. By 1865, there were sixty-five public schools in Harford County and the same number of teachers. The schoolhouses were generally built by local people, often volunteers, and contained the bare essentials. Teachers' salaries ranged from sixty to seventy-five dollars per term. There were no public high schools and very little funding available for county education. In 1870, the Harford County School Board complained that the county commissioners refused to give it the twenty-cent levy required by state law and provided ten cents instead. The school board nevertheless continued acquisitioning property and initiating school construction projects. In Bel Air, the board received the deed to the property at the intersection of Main Street and Bond Street from Herman Stump Jr. The board built a one-room school on the property for white children that operated there until 1883, when it was moved to Hays Street and used for black pupils. Segregation in county schools continued until 1966.

In 1870, there were three standard building plans specifying building size and materials. Plans ranged from twenty-four by twenty-four feet to twenty-four by thirty-seven feet (for a two-teacher school). Each school included a raised platform for the teacher, a blackboard and a stove. John Lingan, the builder of the Bel Air School, failed to include two windows in the front of the building and was penalized and required to add the requisite windows.

The school board determined the school curriculum and required each student to take all subjects listed, basing promotions on a written examination. By 1886, the commissioners had added grades eight and nine to the system. The first curriculum approved for the Bel Air School was as follows:

Seventh Grade: Algebra, Natural Philosophy, English, Latin, Bookkeeping, Composition, Declamation and English History.

Eighth Grade: Geometry, Physiology, English, Literature, Latin, Greek and Ancient History.

Ninth Grade: Trigonometry, Surveying, Astronomy, Latin, Greek, Mental and Moral Philosophy and the Constitution of the United States. The study of the metric system was also recommended.

At this time, the Bel Air Academy (1814–1886) provided education for students who wanted to go beyond elementary school. There were about six separate academies in the area with local trustees appointed by the governor. Each received some funding from the state.

The Bel Air Academy, incorporated by the state in 1811, was without a home until 1814, when Thomas Hays advanced the school $1,064 and let it use an unfinished stone building that he planned to use as a still. The school moved to its final location on Pennsylvania Avenue the next year. The Reverend Reuben Davis became the first principal of the school,

Bel Air Academy was one of the earliest schools in the county, providing educational opportunities for young boys able to pay the tuition. Many of the students went on to distinguished careers in law, medicine and government. *Courtesy of the Town of Bel Air.*

which had two classrooms, one on the first floor, with a laboratory in the back of the room and another on the second floor. As was the practice of the day, there was a raised platform at the head of each classroom. Reverend Davis, known to be a strong disciplinarian, also had a bundle of rods on the platform so as not to spoil the boys in his charge. His reputation as a disciplinarian brought "bad boys" from Maryland and surrounding states there to be educated alongside Harford's scholars. Out-of-town students boarded in the village. Many of the academy students went on to prominent careers in law, medicine and government. The academy limited instruction to boys only. There were a few private schools in Bel Air that provided instruction for girls, but the curriculum was quite different, focusing on household skills, sewing and painting.

With the concern about overcrowding and the need to consolidate numerous one- and two-room schools, the school board initiated condemnation proceedings for property on Gordon Street that eventually became the home of both the Bel Air High and Elementary Schools, but before the proceedings reached the courts, the property

The Bel Air Elementary School, located on Gordon Street, was one of the first brick schools in the county. *Courtesy of the Town of Bel Air.*

owner and the school board reached an agreement on the sale of the property. Again, the board awarded John Lingan the contract to build the new four-room school, which he had completed by March 1883 at a cost of $4,356. By 1897, the board approved an addition of four rooms at a cost of $3,850. Thus began the school consolidation effort, which brought numerous new problems to the school system. Perhaps the greatest hurdle was funding. The general public was not yet convinced of the necessity for higher taxes for public education.

Just getting to the existing schools was a major problem. There was no bus system, and many of the roads in the county were still unpaved. It soon became evident that a horse and wagon, generally called the "Kid Wagon," was needed. Farmers provided transportation for students using a horse and wagon, with one of the older students designated as a driver. Finally, in 1912, a small sum became available through the county to provide transportation, and the state adopted compulsory education legislation in 1916, requiring students to attend classes until age thirteen. Meanwhile, in 1899, the school board adopted regulations "that in the future, a female teacher's marriage shall be construed as her resignation, and no married lady shall be eligible to teach without a special permit from the Board."

In 1911, Saint Margaret's Catholic Church opened a parochial elementary school on the corner of Hickory Avenue and Pennsylvania Avenue in a building donated by Octavius Norris, a lawyer locally known as Judge Norris. He and his brother constructed an impressive three-story home on the corner of Pennsylvania Avenue. They were from the area but actually lived elsewhere. Both were unmarried. Father Frederick, the pastor at Saint Margaret's, knew them well and approached them, noting that the men were getting up in age and had no heirs and that the building would really help the newly formed church. Judge Norris agreed to give the building to Saint Margaret's on the condition that it be used for a school and convent.

On Easter Sunday 1911, Father Frederick officially thanked Judge Norris for his generosity and introduced the three nuns from the School Sisters of Notre Dame who were to operate the school. The sisters arrived that Easter weekend on the Ma & Pa train. They quickly settled in and started classes on Monday, May 1, with forty-three pupils in grades one to six. The nuns lived on the second floor of the house until the church built a new school, with eight grades, at its present location in 1927. The sisters then moved to the Wright house next door to the new school.

The Bel Air Library

As early as 1885, a group of Bel Air residents, calling themselves the Shakespeare Club, developed plans to start the Bel Air Circulating Library. Fundraising started with a minstrel show at the courthouse, with ballads, dances, sketches, etc. The group then started the library and reading rooms in a small building near the courthouse. Advertisements described the reading rooms as "a place where young men could always find comfortable rooms in which to read, play games and smoke." Use of the rooms was free, and "people from the country could go there to rest or meet their friends, with the assurance that they are entirely welcome." The Saint Andrew's Society of the Emmanuel Church and the circulating library sponsored the reading rooms. The Ladies' Auxiliary operated the rooms, which were open each day from 10:00 a.m. to 1:00 p.m. and from 4:00 to 6:00 p.m. Thus began the library's nomadic existence, moving from rooms near the courthouse, to the second floor of a tailor shop, to an old home, to the armory, to a former church and, eventually, to its site on Hickory Avenue. It was constantly expanding to meet the community's needs. For a short time, it was totally abandoned; thus, when Edwin Booth's will specified a donation to the Bel Air Circulating Library, it was no longer in existence, and the town commissioners erected the courthouse fountain instead.

As with most ventures, funding was always a problem. To assist local library needs, in 1902, the newly formed Maryland State Library Commission initiated a traveling library. Communities could request sets of books "on the application of at least three responsible citizens of the vicinity." Books were sent by the case, about thirty-five books to a case at a cost of fifty cents to cover transportation costs. Bel Air requested a greater number of traveling libraries than any other town in the state. Patrons initially focused on fiction and Shakespeare, but over time more diversified subjects became popular. In 1909, the field secretary of the library commission traveled to the county on the Ma & Pa and asked that members of the community meet her to discuss developing a more permanent library. In some places, no one showed up, but in Bel Air, she met with the historical society, which offered to help establish a library for all county citizens and require no subscription fees. The committee included Mrs. H. Stump, Mrs. Richard Dallam, Charles T. Wright and J. Alexis Shriver.

This meeting led to the establishment of a library run by Mrs. Otho Scott Lee in a two-room space above Mr. Bull's tailor shop on Main Street, opposite the post office. By 1913, the library had 815 volumes, all classified according to the Dewey Decimal system. Most of the library's support came from membership dues, donations and entertainments. Eventually, the collection outgrew this small area and moved to the armory in 1918. The county, recognizing the importance of the library to the community, agreed to donate $100 in aid in 1926—although small, it was a beginning. Shortly after that, the library moved to a house on Main Street, finally owning its building for the first time. It was not until 1945 that the state took over the library system. A state law passed requiring counties to appropriate at least two cents of their tax rate for a local library. Prior to this, all local libraries were private. Eventually, with a combination of tax dollars and bond issues, as well as a donation of land from the Town of Bel Air, the library found a permanent home. Guest speaker John Dos Passos, a distinguished nationally and internationally known author, opened the ceremonies celebrating the new beginning for the library and the community. The library system continued to grow, experiencing several expansions, but the building still remains on the same site at Hickory Avenue at Pennsylvania Avenue.

Bel Air Volunteer Fire Company

After the devastating courthouse fire in 1858 and several lesser fires, some local residents decided the time had come to organize a fire company. In 1890, the Bel Air Fire and Salvage Company became a reality. Like the library, this venture experienced difficulty with funding and finding a permanent location. Two early locations are cited, one on Gordon Street and another directly behind the jail on Main Street. The only equipment was a hand-pulled hose reel. Eventually, the fire company purchased a Ford truck. After yet another disastrous fire in 1923, which destroyed the Worthington property on Hickory Avenue, the company reorganized as the Bel Air Volunteer Fire Company and purchased a Seagraves Fire truck.

In 1940, the company found a new home in the garage building on the east side of Bond Street between Pennsylvania Avenue and Lee Street. Volunteers provided the money and manpower to remodel the building. Soon, it became obvious that this building was also too small to handle the new equipment needed to meet the needs of an expanding population. This time, the company traded the site to Harford County for the County Roads Building on the east side of Hickory Avenue (then Dallam Avenue) near Churchville Road. The fire company is still there, although the original County Roads Building is long gone.

Over the years, the station underwent major expansions and redevelopment to meet the needs of modern equipment and the local population. Today, several new stations are located in areas around the town to meet the growing needs of the community. To put this in perspective, the average number of calls in the 1950s was 300 per year; by 2000, these calls had increased to a total of 6,100 calls per year. The Bel Air Volunteer Fire Company is now one of the largest volunteer fire companies in Maryland.

Another major change is the way firefighters are called to a fire. In the early days, a hand-rung bell would let volunteers know of a fire or other emergency. Bel Air's fire company purchased its bell from McShane Foundry in Baltimore. The bell was placed on the courthouse because it was the highest location in town. When a call came, the bell would ring six times for an out-of-town fire and twelve times for a town fire. Once telephone service became common, residents would call the operator to report a fire, and the operator would have the fire bell rung. This was the case until 1939, when the county bought a fire siren. Today, firefighters are notified by pagers and phones. The original bell is now on display at the Hickory Avenue firehouse.

The Police Department

The government always provided for a county sheriff, and later the town added a police department; however, the form of this protection changed radically over the years. Until Bel Air incorporated, and for some time after that, the county sheriff provided police protection for all citizens. However, soon the town board recognized the need for a town police service and appointed a bailiff, who worked with a county-appointed constable. Eventually, an "extra man" was hired to help the bailiff, thereby constituting the first town police force. Over time, the police department expanded, and by 1939 it had acquired its first police car, a Plymouth. For a time, the police operated out of a booth in front of the courthouse. Later, they rented an office in the old Stagmer's Hotel building at the corner of Main Street and Courtland Street. The office moved to the newly constructed town hall on Hickory Avenue in the 1960s and remains there today. The police force is much larger and much more sophisticated now but still works closely with the county sheriff's office and other police services within the county.

AMUSEMENTS AND SPORTS/FUN AND GAMES

As the community grew and new technology provided residents with more leisure time, Bel Air embraced many forms of entertainment not possible earlier. These ranged from theater, movies, baseball and boxing to amateur productions, Lyceum and Chataugua meetings and the ever-popular racetrack. People came from all over the county to participate, taking away lasting memories. Before movies or theaters, the courthouse provided the center for entertainment in Bel Air. Edwin Booth's 1850 courthouse performance is memorialized in a mural at the Bel Air Post Office. It was the most famous of many theatrical productions, concerts and lectures that took place at the courthouse. Then, in 1886, the Masonic Temple opened with a stage and hall large enough for many different types of community events. This immediately became the preferred venue for such productions, as well as public and invitation dances, amateur theatricals, local reviews and road shows. Miss Ada Hadell, with Ms. Ethel Castel on piano, taught scores of young Belairians to dance in the lodge. Dances included the "scandalous waltz" and other dances of the day. Then, in 1915, the armory opened, providing another opportunity for dances, shows and graduation ceremonies. One such event was the production of *Stage Door* in 1940 by the Edwin Booth Dramatic Guild. George Van Bibber, a local artist, and Bill Putnam, the manager of the Argonne Theater, designed the scenery for the show, and local actors played all parts. World War II brought the demise of the theater group as actors found themselves recruited for the conflict, and the armory reverted to full-time military operation.

The amateur productions at the armory provided both entertainment and rivalry, as the regulars competed for prizes and recognition. Two of the groups went on to become crowd favorites. The McComas Brothers Quartet reportedly wowed the crowds regularly with its barbershop quartet sounds. Stanley, the tenor, and Emory, the bass (who reportedly could make the windows rattle with his melodious voice), owned and operated the McComas Hardware, Lumber and Coal business next to the Ma & Pa Railroad depot. Walter and Charles were lawyers. When Walter died, the brothers would invite anyone brave enough to sing with them to come forward to fill his spot. Earl Burkins, the owner of the Argonne Theater, often filled this place, but very few people were daring enough to take on this challenge. The other main attraction in these amateur productions was the Getz Brothers. Again, the brothers provided comedy, music and just plain fun for the audiences, who kept coming back for the entertainment and the competition. Another popular attraction was the minstrel show. In the 1930s, the armory regularly hosted traveling minstrel shows for local audiences.

In the early 1900s, a new source of entertainment arrived with the introduction of the silent movies. Bel Air's first movie house, called the *Busy Moon*, was located across from the old Courtland Hardware store on South Main Street. This was the era of black-and-white silent movies, complete with piano accompaniment. The building was a simple wooden hall with a small screen on a stage and one aisle between rows of dark reddish veneered wooden seats. These were slanted toward the screen, and arc lamps with frosted glass and brass fans hung from the white bead board ceiling to provide light and air. There was no main feature. The single hand-cranked projector held only one reel, so at the end of each reel there was an intermission allowing viewers to race to the entrance for a bag of roasted peanuts, whose shells lined the floor in mounds like snowdrifts.

In George Van Bibber's writings, he describes one of the piano players, a Mr. Hoffman, who could play music appropriate to whatever action or emotion unfolded as the stories and the flickering images appeared on the screen. His partner, Mr. Emault, a hefty man with a walrus mustache and a good reach, dealt with the more "obstreperous males" in the audience. The end of each ten-cent show featured the descent of a pastel coloring of a sparsely clad female lying on a crescent moon, hence the name "Busy Moon." After a few years, the movie house moved to North Main Street near Pennsylvania Avenue.

About the same time, a member of the Reckord family hired the armory and added a piano, a screen and a projector to open a second movie house. This theater lasted only about a year, with performances three or four times a week. Meanwhile, Earle Burkins purchased the Busy Moon. He was a World War I veteran and fought at the Battle of the Argonne. He renamed the theater the Argonne, commemorating this famous battle. He hired Irving Smith, a high school music teacher, to play piano music appropriate to the scene showing on the screen. Mr. Smith often brought along gifted students to try their hand at this.

In 1928, Mr. Burkins bought the Malcolm Stewart property, located somewhat closer to Pennsylvania Avenue on Main Street. He then built an ornate Georgian theater with a wide gallery, a lobby framed by a pair of mock marble Tuscan columns and a very expensive pipe organ. Within a year, talkies replaced silent movies, making the organ somewhat obsolete, but the theater remained the place to go in Bel Air. The name changed to the Bel Air Theater when Major Burkins retired and sold to a new owner. Over the ensuing years, the movie house was the center of activity not only for movies but also for many other activities. The basement was home to American Legion Post #39 until it purchased the old Webster property on Hickory Avenue in 1947.

The large basement area of the theater provided space for the ever-popular boxing matches that the American Legion sponsored before the matches moved to the armory arena. The armory boxing bouts were well advertised. Entrance fees ranged from fifty cents for general seating to seventy-five cents for reserved seating, and of course, ladies were free. The Chesterfield Cigarette Girls served as ushers. Various clubs throughout the county put up contenders. For example, in one of the advertised matches, the Easterwood Democratic Club and the Cross Country Club each sponsored contenders fighting against Havre de Grace fighters. Bouts often listed contenders from Edgewood Arsenal and Fort Hoyle. Local promoters brought in people from across the county boasting as many as twenty-eight rounds of boxing in a night. One local fighter, Warrenell

(Boom Boom) Lester, went on to become the state champion, once as the light heavyweight and a second time as the heavyweight contender. In 1954, he won the Armed Forces light heavyweight championship and the National AAU light heavyweight championship at Boston Garden. His local fights always sold out, whether at Bainbridge Naval Center, Harford County Fairgrounds or the armory. He fought in Yankee Stadium in 1955 and was inducted into the Maryland Boxing Hall of Fame in 1981. After retiring from the ring, Mr. Lester ran an athletic center on Bond Street, training many young boxers for the future. He inspired these young people with his talent and sharp wit.

These were the days before television, so entertainment took many forms, including shows, movies, boxing, racing and particularly baseball, which was a major sport in Bel Air. Initially, the Bel Air Nine played on a diamond at the Bel Air Racetrack. Later, they became part of the Susquehanna League, competing with teams from throughout the region. In the 1880s, newspapers throughout Harford County touted local amateur and semiprofessional teams. In 1920, the Susquehanna League formed with teams from Aberdeen, Bel Air and Havre de Grace, as well as Cecil County teams and an Oxford, Pennsylvania team. There were a number of in-state leagues for younger players, giving young boys a chance to develop and eventually play in the Susquehanna League. Bel Air was part of the Bel Air Harford Road League.

The Susquehanna League was considered a semiprofessional league, and some teams brought in players from a wide geographical area, but Bel Air and Aberdeen fielded only local players. Since Bel Air did not field a team regularly, some local players participated with the Hickory team when a Bel Air team was not fielded. One of these Bel Air players was John Schafer, who both played for and managed the Hickory team. He also managed the Bel Air "County Seaters" in 1947. By all accounts, he was an excellent fielder and an outstanding hitter. Some games of the Susquehanna League attracted as many as 2,500 fans. Mr. Schafer went on to become Councilman Shafer, serving on the Harford County Council for many years. His fellow councilman, Lehman Spry, teased him regularly with barbs like: "He's always assumed he's Ty Cobb."

Of course, men and boys were not the only ones enamored of the game. A March 23, 1929 headline in the *Baltimore Sun* pronounced, "Goucher Girls with Knickers Startled Staid Bel Air Citizens." Thirty girls from Goucher

College rented the Country Club Inn for the weekend. The students arrived via autobus with their bobbed hair and knickers for a house party in Bel Air. The girls played baseball in front of the inn and then took a hike, apparently shocking some locals. This was, of course, in the days when ladies did not wear trousers or cut their hair and certainly did not play baseball.

The Chataugua and Lyceum

At the other end of the spectrum, the Chataugua provided the cultural entertainment craved by many people in the county who missed the elevated entertainment available in the cities. Traveling outside the county for entertainment was quite arduous, so at least twice a year entertainment came to Bel Air in the form of the Chataugua in the summer and the Lyceum in the winter.

These programs attracted as many as five hundred people from across the county. Each year in the late 1910s and early 1920s, the Chataugua tents went up on the Bel Air Elementary School property on Gordon Street as soon as school ended for the year. For one week, singers, instrumentalists, magicians, lecturers, jugglers and poets shared the stage, entertaining citizens from across the county. One of the more noted speakers was William Jennings Bryant. The talent and programs were organized by high-minded people at their spiritual headquarters on Lake Chataugua in upstate New York. Each year, the week would end with a Grand Finale—a Gilbert & Sullivan operetta such as *The Mikado* or *HMS Pinafore*. This entertainment could not compete with movies and radio, so it was nearly lost, but the Chataugua continues in some places even today.

This was of course a summer event. In the winter, the Lyceum would provide similar inspiration with lectures, musical performances, concerts and general entertainment at the Masonic Temple Hall and later at the armory. Programs were modestly priced and well attended. As an example, according to the April 3, 1897 issue of the *Democratic Ledger*, the upcoming season included a series of lectures organized by the Friday Night Lecture Club with such noted programs as: "A Tour of Scotland" by D. Howard Haman of the Baltimore Bar; "Napoleon the King of Warriors" by Charles E. Guthrie of Baltimore; "The Reign of the Frost King" by Professor H.A. Hazen of the Washington Weather Bureau; "The Last Day of Pompeii" by Howard W. Ennis of Washington, D.C.;

"A Forecast of the Weather" by Professor Willis L. Moore, chief of the Washington Weather Bureau; and "Marvels of Modern Surgery" by Bel Air native Dr. J.M.T. Finney of the Johns Hopkins Hospital in Baltimore.

On Saturday nights, Bel Air was a bustling place; people from the countryside would come in to shop, visit, play Bingo, go to the Ladies' Auxiliary or just watch the entertainment from the front of the courthouse. There was no television and limited alternative entertainment. The people were their own entertainment.

Bel Air Racetrack

The Bel Air Racetrack was a major tourist attraction and entertainment destination for Bel Air residents for many years. The local inns would fill to capacity during racing season. The track was one mile north of Baltimore Pike, just east of Tollgate Road. It consisted of one hundred acres laid out by G.G. Curtis in the 1870s. The first Harford County Fair held in 1874 included exhibitions, horse, cattle, homemade goods, paintings, a jousting tournament and a fair queen, much like today's county fairs. There was a grandiose framed gateway with a ticket office and a clubhouse located on the west side. A beautiful grandstand was

The Bel Air Racetrack featured a half-mile track with grandstands, a racetrack and fairgrounds. It was a major source of entertainment for generations of local citizens and tourists.

added in 1937. On fair days, agrarian interests mixed with a general carnival atmosphere, complete with a midway and games of chance. Race days were more focused with some very dramatic contests. In addition to the Thoroughbreds that raced on the half-mile circuit, local farmers competed with their fastest horses, although not necessarily Thoroughbreds, at what was known as the gyp circuit.

Bel Air Racetrack spurred many legends; one was the story of Charles Burns. At his death in 1927, the *Baltimore Afro American* newspaper noted that "Charlie" spent forty years as a breaker of driving horses in Bel Air. Many of the Thoroughbreds that drew the carriages of aristocratic families in the days of the carriage and coach were trained by his hand. He was a racer, trainer and ace of the dirt track when sulky races were the rage. His own horse, Coolie, had his greatest rival in Plowboy, owned by Major General Milton A. Reckord of the Maryland National Guard. After several years, the rivalry ended with the Burns entry unconquered.

This was a beautiful racetrack with expansive turns and races to suit every interest. Betting made these races all the more interesting. The track was relatively flat and slightly shorter than Laurel or Bowie. There was a magnificent spreading oak in the infield providing a breeze and some shade. When the races were in town or the county fair was in operation, locals deserted downtown for the excitement of the day. Crowds descended on Bel Air from up and down the East Coast, with attendance sometimes ranging between 6,500 and 15,000. Usually, there were two standard races and then the steeplechase. Several additional races followed, including harness and sulky races in the 1920s and even small chassis car races in the 1930s.

As described by George Van Bibber:

> In one such contest, a car didn't stick to the dirt track and struck down some spectators, badly injuring them. They had a sheet over the poor lad who seemed dead. A local doctor thought he'd better take a look. The result was that the boy was rushed to the hospital after word of his death had begun to circulate in the community. Thus his nickname thereafter was "Ghost."

When not serving as a racing center or county fair site, the racetrack became home to the annual "Field Meet." Students from across the county competed in the one-hundred-yard dash and other track events, as well as the Dodge Ball Competition.

In the 1940s, the racetrack found its way into the center of a dispute between Governor Lane and George P. Mahoney when the governor replaced Mahoney as chairman of the Racing Commission. Mahoney claimed he was replaced because he tried to "clean up" the "Sport of Kings," citing his attacks against race fixing and the practice of doping horses. He claimed to have caught mobsters as they tried to substitute a ringer, Don't Delay, for Ole Flo at Bel Air Racetrack, but the jockey who could corroborate this mysteriously drove off a West Virginia road before he could be questioned.

In 1951, the track owner, G. Ray Bryson, requested more racing dates but was turned down. At the same time, a new harness track, Baltimore Raceway, opened on Glenn L. Martin Boulevard and Pulaski Highway with more land, more seating and more parking. One by one, the smaller tracks closed as the mile tracks bought up the racing dates. When Mr. Bryson died in 1957, the track declined precipitously. The final death knell came when Jerry Hoffberger persuaded the state legislature to transfer Bel Air's race dates to Pimlico, Laurel and Bowie, effectively eliminating racing in Bel Air.

The racetrack was sold in 1960, later becoming the home of Harford Mall, spelling the end of an era.

Murder and Mayhem

As the town moved from the nineteenth century to the twentieth, most residents basked in the progress of the times. Homes and businesses now had electricity and town water and many had automobiles or even telephones. There was a sense of prosperity. As described in the *Baltimore Sun* in an article about Stevenson A. Williams, the Republican candidate for governor, in October 1903:

> *Bel Air is a town of beautiful homes that shelter a refined and cultured people. Alighting from the train at the north end of the village, the visitor finds himself treading the long main street: that is, if he does not take one of the half dozen vehicles whose services may be secured at the*

station. It is pleasanter to walk along the wide, well shaded thoroughfare and enjoy the peaceful homelike atmosphere of the place. First, there are several modest frame stores, and one or two were imposing factories. Farther along the way is lined with comfortable dwellings, and here and there a church. None of these homes is pretentious in the way of making an ostentatious commodious display of wealth. They are comfortable surrounded by lawn spaces of greater or less extent with shade trees, shrubbery and with flowers and with inviting porches where hammocks and easy chairs indicate restful enjoyment of the long summer evenings.

The *Sun* reporter emphasized that Mr. Williams was in the contest out of a sense of duty. He had never really sought elected office, having a very full and satisfying career in Bel Air. Mr. Williams lost the election. He then continued with his legal practice and his duties as president of the Harford National Bank. While this idyllic vision of Bel Air held true for many, there was also another side of the story.

As the new century began, papers throughout the country broadcast the story of the "Lynching Affair." On a Sunday in March 1900, Ms. Annie McIlvaine, an older woman who lived on the outskirts of Bel Air and made a living selling herbal remedies, was awakened about 4:00 a.m. with a loud knock at her door. Seeing a man standing there, she opened the window and asked what he wanted. The man, Lewis Harris, claimed he needed medication for a toothache. Ms. McIlvaine opened her kitchen window and handed out a vile of medication. She then waited for a few minutes until all was quiet and opened the door, planning to run for a neighbor's house. As she left the house, Mr. Harris attacked her, and a violent struggle ensued. She screamed loudly and was able to attract the attention of a "colored man," Al Jackson, who lived nearby.

Mr. Jackson grabbed his pistol and ran to the door, firing a shot toward the attacker, at which time Mr. Harris ran away. Ms. McIlvaine ran to the sheriff's office and stayed there until the morning, when Sheriff Kinhart accompanied her to her home and found the attacker's hat on the ground outside the house. He recognized it immediately as one his hostler, Lewis Harris, wore. He immediately went in search of Mr. Harris and found him in front of Morgan's store. Meanwhile, news spread throughout the town, and crowds formed near the jail. Ms. McIlvaine identified Mr. Harris as her attacker, and the local doctor, Dr. E. Hall Richardson, examined Mr. Harris and found wounds on his hands indicating he had been in a skirmish. The sheriff scheduled a hearing for the next day but found that, with the large crowds outside the jail, it was not safe to take the prisoner out of the jail. The crowd was apparently aroused by a recent incident near Stemmers Run in the Aberdeen area, where a black individual was acquitted of attacking a young lady.

At about 11:30 p.m., some fifty people, many of whom were masked, reached the jail and demanded the keys. When the sheriff refused, someone discharged a pistol, and a fusillade followed. A blacksmith's sledgehammer pounded against the rear door of the jail. By this time, many in the crowd had begun to scatter, fearing stray bullets, while others forced the prisoner down Main Street toward Churchville Road. The mob leaders shouted that they needed to take him out of town. The mob rushed to the Archer farm just outside the town boundaries (the old almshouse property at Shamrock). Mr. Harris offered no resistance and repeated, "If I did it, I was drunk and didn't know what I was doing."

By this time, the frenzy was such that the men grabbed Harris and threw the rope that was around his neck over a tree branch. They lifted him up, only to have the branch break under his weight. Again, the mob tried another branch, lifting him about five feet from the ground; to make sure the deed was done, shots were fired into his abdomen. The crowd then dispersed, and the town was as quiet as if nothing had occurred. Later investigations into the matter found that the sheriff and his deputies were blameless in the incident, and no charges were ever filed against the perpetrators. It was noted that no one could identify them because of their masks.

V
MODERN WAR COMES TO BEL AIR

WILSON'S WAR

With the turn of the century, the local general stores, Carver & Price and J. Woodley Richardson's, did a booming business. One source describes "the coffee grinders painted fire engine red, with the aroma of the grinds permeating the stores. Without seeing it you knew that the smoked herring was here and molasses waited. There were huge drums of orange colored cheese that the shopkeeper cut like a cake." The streets were still lined with hitching posts and slate walks from the quarries in Delta and Cardiff. But things were definitely changing. The liveries, blacksmiths and hitching posts were disappearing as the automobile began overtaking the horse and wagon. The excitement of the new technological innovations—electricity, the telephone, hard surface roads—was somewhat dampened by outside forces. The Mexican War saw local boys called to service as troops marched down Main Street to the Ma & Pa Railroad depot and were transported to the National Guard Armory in Baltimore for assignment. Still, few thought they would be called for yet another European war. But inevitably, the war came, and the country would never be the same.

The Jackson Guard originally consisted of about eighty men. In 1888, it became the First Regiment National Guard, Company D, and remained in continuous existence until federalized in October 1917. Through these transitions, the guardsmen used a site on Main Street and some local farm

The Bel Air Armory, built in 1915, was the home of the Maryland National Guard in Bel Air until 2010. It is now a community center.

fields for training. In 1915, the state authorized the construction of several new National Guard headquarters, one of which would be located in Bel Air. In response to an architectural design competition, John B. Hamme of York, Pennsylvania, submitted the gray crenellated tower design, reminiscent of a Scottish Gothic Revival castle, that became the winning entry for Bel Air's Armory. The imposing Port Deposit granite structure became the home of Company D of the First Maryland Regiment of the Maryland National Guard. Company D had already served in the coal strike in western Maryland, the Spanish-American War and against Pancho Villa in the Mexican border conflict. Now, with their new home just completed, the federal government called the troops to serve in France in World War I. While the armory became a center of military activities in Bel Air, the president planned an even greater military presence in Harford County. On October 20, 1917, soon after America's entry into World War I, an act of Congress and two proclamations by President Woodrow Wilson created Aberdeen Proving Ground, eventually taking about 25 percent of Harford's land area for military purposes.

The war had a direct impact on many local families. This was the very beginning of Milton Reckord's years of service. A local boy, he graduated from Bel Air High School in 1896 and went on to work at the family mill on North Main Street. By 1900, he was listed in the census as an electrician, helping to operate the electric service to the mill and the Town of Bel Air. He managed the workers his father assembled to clear the path, plant the poles and string the wires for this nascent electric service. In 1907, Reckord took over the mill at his father's death, turning it over to managers as his military career progressed and eventually selling the

COL. M. ATCHISON RECKORD Of Belair. Commands The 115th Infantry. "Baltimore's Own. Made Of Men From First, Fourth And Fifth

The Bel Air Armory is named for Lieutenant General Milton Reckord, a Bel Air native, who served with distinction in both World War I and World War II.

business to H. Smith Michael, the grandfather of the current owner.

Reckord's sixty-four-year military career began in 1901 at the age of twenty-one, when he enlisted as a private in Company D of the Maryland National Guard (then the Jackson Guard). He rose through the ranks quickly. By 1916, he had received a commission as major, to take command of the 2nd Battalion, 1st Maryland Infantry, which deployed to the Mexican border under the command of General Pershing. When the 29th Division was created on the eve of World War I, Reckord was given command of one of its regiments, the 115th Infantry, which saw combat during the Meuse-Argonne offensive. A *Sun* reporter, Raymond Tompkins, described him at the time as a "great soldier…a small, slender, snappy man—all old regular officer."

It soon became obvious that the expanding war in Europe could not be avoided here at home. The National Guard received its first order from the governor on March 22, 1917, just a week before the president's April 2, 1917 formal request for war. The guard's first assignment, led by Bel Air attorney Captain Robert H. Archer, called for eighty-five men to protect the railroad bridges in Havre de Grace. Orders specified that the guard "arrest everybody about whom there is in the least suspicion and to shoot on site anyone who tries to destroy the bridges." To ensure the assignment went well, Major Reckord asked Havre de Grace innkeepers not to serve alcohol to any men in uniform. Although the mission was successful and resulted in good publicity and new recruits, the men were pleased to be replaced by units of the Fourth Regiment a few weeks later.

Shortly after this, Congress declared war against the German Empire, and guard troops under Captain Archer received orders to defend the Montebello filtration plant in Baltimore. Another prominent Harford County native, Lieutenant Millard Tydings, commanded thirty men sent to Loch Raven Water Works. Tydings, a lawyer from Havre de Grace, had joined the guard in 1916 at the urging of his friend Milton Reckord and helped to recruit a platoon of approximately twenty men from Aberdeen and Havre de Grace. Because of his earlier military training at the University of Maryland, he was promoted to second lieutenant and platoon commander. He later told the story that he had no sooner signed these recruits than war broke out, and Reckord called him to say he had not yet turned in the paperwork for the recruits. If they wanted to back out, he would understand. Tydings contacted all the men, and each said he was ready to take on the Huns and wanted to stay with the guard. On September 10, 1917, Harford's Company D marched across the city to Baltimore's Camden Station for the first leg of their journey to France and the Great War.

In May 1917, Congress passed the Selective Service Act requiring all males ages twenty-one to thirty to register for possible military service. This later changed to ages eighteen to forty-five. At that time, the entire country had 110,000 soldiers and 200,000 guardsmen. By the end of the war, 4.8 million men had served. There were no procedures in place, no preset rules to deal with such mobilization. The state formed the Maryland Council of Defense to help plan for the state's war needs and responsibilities. Bel Air attorney Stevenson A. Williams served on the council and chaired Harford County's Council of Defense. A military census committee, chaired by Bel Air attorney Thomas A. Robinson, organized a list of all potential draftees. Subsequently, the governor appointed three local men as the Harford County Draft Board: John Robinson, the clerk of the circuit court; Dr. Walter Kirk, an active practitioner and part-time health officer; and Robert Atkins, the county sheriff. The board then organized the draft registration, decided on exemptions and oversaw the selection of men to fill the county's draft quota.

To encourage enrollment, the board planned a patriotic festival at the Bel Air Armory enticing men to "serve in a Maryland Regiment with men from your own community." Boy Scouts played music and shouted scout yells; Bel Air High School students attended, listening to patriotic speeches. Judge Harlan of the Council for Defense and local attorney Samuel Bradford, son of the former governor Augustus Bradford, gave keynote addresses. By day's end, over two thousand men had signed up for the draft.

The Bel Air Women's Council of Defense also organized community assistance, such as patriotic send-offs at the Bel Air Armory. These included opening prayers, speeches followed by a crowd accompanying the men to the Ma & Pa Railroad station, where the draftees took the train to Baltimore. Each draftee received a trench mirror and comfort kit.

Dr. John M.T. Finney grew up in Bel Air and attended the Bel Air Academy before attending college at Princeton. In 1888, after serving at the Massachusetts General Hospital for eighteen months, Dr. William Halsted invited him to join the faculty of the new Johns Hopkins Medical School, where many of the nation's best doctors received instruction under the renowned "Big Four." At the start of the war, Dr. Finney became director and chief surgeon of Johns Hopkins Base Hospital #18. Now Major Finney, he led the Hopkins entourage to Bezoilles on the River Meuse in June 1917, establishing a fully staffed medical center with a capacity for one thousand patients. By war's end, Dr. Finney was a brigadier general. He returned to Baltimore to resume his civilian career.

Bel Air residents John Abell Hunter and Elizabeth Hawkins Harlan, a Red Cross nurse, served in this unit. Ms. Harlan was the daughter of Judge William Harlan and Dr. Finney's cousin. After the war, she received a citation for Gallantry in Action along with five other nurses for service at the 103rd Field Hospital. On July 15, 1918, while under an enemy air raid, "they refused to seek shelter, but remained bravely at their posts administering to the wounded." On her return, Ms. Harlan became

Harford County's first public visiting nurse, providing needed care and instruction at schools, homes and worksites. In addition to administering rudimentary physical exams to schoolchildren, Miss Harlan provided maternal and infant care for women, tested for TB, gave directions in sanitation and hygiene, sought to control communicable diseases and provided general nursing for a variety of ailments and injuries. Her office was at the Bel Air Armory until 1920, when she left her position to marry Dr. John Cushman Lyman, with whom she had served in France.

Health concerns also played a significant role in the war's mobilization effort as many of the soldiers succumbed to disease even before leaving for Europe. These young farmers, having grown up on solitary farms with little outside contact, were suddenly forced into large groups of people with various diseases. They had little immunity to these infectious diseases, and sickness soon followed. Making matters worse, Spanish flu spread among the troops, killing many. For those who made it to France, even more treacherous measures awaited. Soldiers faced lethal gas attacks, gunfire and bombs. Private Edward Osborne of Bel Air, at age seventeen, was Harford's youngest soldier. After sustaining a minor injury in France, he died of pneumonia one month before the war's end.

Along with the patriotic fervor and pressures of mobilization, county citizens also found themselves dealing with the economic reality of losing "one of the most important sugar corn and tomato canning areas in the United States" to the U.S. Army's new ordnance facility, Aberdeen Proving Grounds. While Aberdeen citizens faced the most direct effects, Bel Air's canning brokers and financial institutions realized significant impacts; local government felt the loss of tax dollars as the county shrank from 520 square miles to 464 square miles. The quality of life, particularly access to the bay and the Susquehanna's rich fishing and hunting grounds, suffered a severe loss. Estimates showed that at least $700,000 would be lost annually with the army's takeover of 30 miles of shoreline, closing the nation's best duck-hunting sites, and the associated impacts on products from local fisheries. Protests were to no avail.

On October 16, 1917, President Wilson issued a proclamation authorizing the secretary of war "to take over the land." The government appointed four men to fix values of the land being confiscated. Bel Air attorney Thomas A. Robinson was appointed to represent local landowners. The proclamation gave area residents until January 1, 1918, to vacate the premises, along with all of their livestock and belongings. Many had no place to go. It was a traumatic experience dislocating not just landowners but also tenant farmers and workers—people who had lived on this land for generations. Everything had to go because once the buildings and homes were vacated, residents were not allowed to return for any reason. By the war's end, on November 11, 1918, the once rich farming and hunting peninsula was gone, replaced by a major military installation and testing facility.

Civilians were equally impacted by the war. Farm life during World War I was rugged at best. There was no water in the houses—just a pump near the back door—so of course there was no bathroom, no electricity and no furnace. Mary Hall, whose family lived on Broadway, described moving to her family's farm during the war to help her grandfather:

> We had Franklin stoves in the fireplace with registers over them for the heat to go upstairs. Not much did! Pitchers of water stood on the water stands in each bedroom, and bath water was heated on the big kitchen range, where it was poured into a washtub, and we children were bathed according to age, the youngest first, and a little clean water was added in between. During the dreadful flu epidemic of '17–'18, taking care of the sick in those conditions was awful. It was almost impossible to get a doctor or nurses. Lots of people died. A bus was sent to Bel Air to pick up girls and take them to APG for dances. They used an old-time grind-up Victrola. Because of the food shortages, you had to go from place to place to get sugar and flour, but we grew our own fruits and vegetables and hunted rabbit, even ate groundhog.

There were many stories of local service and sacrifice. Everyone wanted to do his part in the "War to End All Wars." Years later, Broadnax Cameron told of his service in the war. His family lived at Joshua's Meadows on Tollgate Road (the former Bond property). The Camerons were a well-respected family from Virginia. Broadnax received his education at Princeton and the University of Virginia. Although he loved architecture and would dabble in it for the rest of his life, he followed his family's wishes and became a lawyer. In 1917, at the age of twenty-one, he volunteered with the American Ambulance Corp in France and served there and in Salonika in the Balkans. He also served in Austin,

Texas, as an air service instructor, providing aircraft engine instruction. After the war, Broadnax married Julia Duryea Spriggs and went on to have three sons: Broadnax Jr., Duryea and George. He founded the law firm of Jacobs and Cameron, practicing in Bel Air for many years. He was the director of Bata Shoe Company and founding trustee, president and treasurer of Harford Day School.

Like most of the men who served, Bel Air's soldiers downplayed their roles, came home and quietly resumed their careers, even though their experiences stayed with them forever. At last the war ended, and the town celebrated with a victory jubilee at the Bel Air Armory on Monday, November 18, 1918. Posters promised a stirring address by the Honorable J. Charles Linthicum and other prominent county speakers. S. Carroll Harrison of Baltimore had served as the overseas secretary during the war. He was on hand to tell the story of his fifteen months at the front. The Aberdeen Proving Ground Band and Bugle Corps played for the occasion, and the McComas Brothers Quartet provided musical entertainment. All families of "Harford Boys in Blue and Khaki are invited as guests of honor."

Similar celebrations heralded the war's end throughout the county. Soldiers returned to their hometowns to parades, banquets and dances. One of the biggest celebrations was reserved for the return of Colonel Reckord. On June 6, 1919, Bel Air's hometown hero was "literally besieged...by friends, each of whom wished to give his hand a warm grasp of welcome." The fire bell rang out welcoming him to the courthouse lawn, where crowds of admirers awaited him. Four years later, on July 13, 1923, a large crowd assembled outside the Bel Air Armory to dedicate a memorial plaque to those Harford County citizens who died in the service of the country during the First World War.

THE GREAT DEPRESSION

For a time after the war, life seemed to return to normal. The 1920s brought a sigh of relief to everyone. Leaving the horrors and depravations of the war years behind, citizens were able to begin rebuilding their lives. There was a new emphasis on education. While the county commissioners remained unsupportive, the three members of the state-appointed Board of Education, with school superintendent C. Milton

Wright and newly elected delegate Mary Risteau, felt strongly that new schools needed to be financed and constructed as soon as possible. They took their case to the county citizens and developed a countywide financing plan that included the sale of bonds. With the help of the county's senior delegate, Millard Tydings, the bond issue passed, setting a precedent for future funding.

In 1924, the county built a new brick high school next to Bel Air Elementary School. Bel Air High opened with eight regular classrooms, a laboratory, typewriters, a special science room and an agricultural program. Classes were expanded to include grades eight through eleven. The original building now became an elementary school for grades one through seven. In 1931, another expansion project added ten more rooms. Still, the schools offered no frills. Music, art, band and most sports remained a dream for the future, but the high school did produce an operetta each year, and Dr. Bird Hopkins volunteered his time and talent to train track students. These track students competed annually at the fairgrounds, attracting thousands of spectators from all over the county as elementary and high school students competed in track, dodge ball and baseball. Three of Bel Air's track stars—Jimmy Kehoe, Ronald Hulsbert and Harford Cronin—went on to be top performers at the University of Maryland. Of course, the highlight of the day was the trip to Bull's store or Richardson's Drugstore after school for sodas, candy or possibly a sundae.

In 1935, construction began on Bel Air's first colored high school with a new building on Hays Street. This was largely due to the efforts of Hannah Moore. Ms. Moore moved from Baltimore City to Bel Air as a young child, shortly after her mother died from yellow fever. Raised on a farm next to Lake Fanny Hill, just south of Bel Air, her father worked for the Durham family. She married in 1906. Ms. Moore and her husband ran the only store for blacks in town, which Mr. Moore started in 1901. He also worked at hotels, traveling to Saratoga with the races. Her brothers trained horses. They purchased several properties in Bel Air, eventually owning thirty-one acres along Baltimore Pike, a portion of which now contains Bel Air High School and Kunkels Automotive. They had six children, all of whom became professionals (one doctor and five teachers). Ms. Moore's passion for education and her business acumen were largely responsible for the development of higher education for black students in Bel Air.

Until the 1930s, black families were forced to arrange schooling outside the county, if at all. Ms. Moore initially met with the school superintendent and asked if the school board would consider building a school for the black students, but she was advised that there was no money for such an endeavor. However, she could contact the Rosenwald Foundation, which was connected to Sears Roebuck and Company. It provided matching funding for black schools throughout the country. Ms. Moore approached the foundation and was able to obtain $900 toward the cost of the school. Ms. Moore personally matched this amount and provided the land for the school; thus began the Bel Air Colored School (in 1922–23) on Hays Street, at a total cost of $8,475. Prior to this, black students had used a hand-me-down one-room school that was no longer used for white students.

The county provided education for black students until the sixth or seventh grades. In 1930, a black high school was established in Havre de Grace, but it took several years before Clayton Stansbury, a black community leader, and the colored PTA, again with help from Ms. Moore, were able to get permission to build an addition to the Bel Air site for a black high school. Ms. Moore donated books for the library, machines for sewing classes and tables and chairs from her business for the kitchen area. Shop classes were actually taught in Ms. Moore's garage on Bond Street. Students from the school went on to become teachers, professional boxers, entrepreneurs and local government employees. In 1950, the county developed the Consolidated School at Hickory, which replaced the Bel Air colored schools until integration was finally adopted by Harford County in the 1960s.

Life seemed to be returning to normal, possibly even a return to good times. Still, there were concerns. Prohibition was hotly discussed. The Eighteenth Amendment, ratified in 1919, outlawed the sale of liquor. Very quickly, bootleggers flourished, and moonshine operations sprouted throughout the county. Legend tells of several local speakeasies, some right across from the courthouse. The federal agents—or revenuers, as the locals called them—used dynamite to destroy a plethora of local stills. In one instance, the *Aegis* described a raid, claiming that "twenty-five gallons of whiskey, fifteen hundred gallons of mash were destroyed by dynamite as was the manufacturing plant. In raids during the past two weeks this was the fifth still found [and destroyed] within the borders of Harford County."

Modern War Comes to Bel Air

Local residents generally reviled the revenuers as unwanted outsiders. In 1923, one report described the sheriff standing on Churchville Road at the entrance to Bel Air with several others on a Thursday morning. All of a sudden, a Buick sedan flew around the corner into another car, forcing it to overturn. Several people fell from the car, and Sheriff Sheridan rushed to the cars when a fight broke out. It turned out that revenuers in the Buick were chasing bootleggers in the other car. The revenue officers explained the situation, arrested the bootleggers and confiscated their "wet goods" before starting off for Baltimore with the culprits. For the next several years, until Prohibition's repeal, the papers were filled with descriptions of raids, still explosions and bootleg liquor stories. The only crime more prevalent at the time was bookmaking, with the sheriff regularly raiding "gambling dens" and arresting bookies.

Farm prices and the economy raised serious concerns, but for a time the Argonne Movie Theater offered escape with features like *Midnight Express* and *The Prairie Wife*. Newly available trucks and automobiles made travel much easier and more entertaining. Frigidaire provided well-attended demonstrations on the new electric refrigerators at the Argonne Theater, promising new work-saving appliances for housewives. There were any number of new timesaving inventions to dazzle the public. New car dealers opened throughout the county seat. Complementing earlier arrivals like Frank MacLean's Ford Agency, the Overland and Willy's Agency opened in 1922. Henry Crocker opened another Ford agency across from the courthouse. He advertised that "the war is over and war prices must go," offering a Ford sedan with an electric starter for $750. David Lee started the Chandler and Dodge dealer on South Main Street in 1921, and A.S. Magness and Son opened the Chrysler/Plymouth dealership at Churchville Road and Main Street. Finally, Howard O' Neill and J. Herbert Hanna started the Chevrolet, Oldsmobile and Cadillac dealership on Bond Street.

New national stores like Woolworths opened on Main Street. New bus service spread rapidly, offering inexpensive rides to other parts of the county and to Baltimore. The Ma & Pa Railroad began to modernize, offering a combination coach and baggage car powered by a gasoline engine, the first of its kind in the country. All of this emphasis on transportation brought with it a terrible increase in vehicular accidents. The newspapers featured stories about fatalities almost every week, many between automobiles and horse and buggies. This led to an outcry for better roads, which became a major issue with the county commissioners, who were hesitant to spend county funds to improve the roads. There was also pressure on them to improve the jail, as frequent breakouts occurred once prisoners realized how easy it was to pick the jail's locks or saw through the window bars. New combination locks did not help, as one career criminal demonstrated by disabling all of them in one afternoon. These constituted day-to-day problems of small-town life, but then disaster struck.

On October 29, 1929, the stock market collapsed. At first, it was deemed a short-term problem. Then, the true picture became visible. Local banks closed. Money grew scarce, and the county, like the rest of the country, began to deal with job losses, homelessness, declining markets and milk prices. The Dairymen's Association held several mass meetings in Bel Air, searching for solutions to falling prices and increased competition. Then a killer drought hit in 1930, destroying many vegetable crops and driving several canning operations out of business. The local water company was unable to increase its needed water supply and went into bankruptcy. Three major fires hit Main Street in the 1930s. First, in 1930, Coale's store was destroyed. Then, in 1931, Hirsch's Men's Store caught fire, ignited by dry cleaning fluid. The store was quickly repaired but caused considerable damage. One of the most devastating fires hit the Bel Air Presbyterian Church on North Main Street, but because they were able to save the original church plans, the church was rebuilt according to its original design.

Remarkably, people remained resilient and drew together to help one another. Local citizens organized "relief committees." Bel Air's committee initially raised $1,000 and used the money to help people find work or, if they were in dire need, to provide funds. Local teachers raised $900 and turned it over to the relief effort. The state American Legion led by Bel Air's Robert Archer announced in 1932 that it would work in local communities to help people find work. President Roosevelt's election brought some hope with the numerous programs designed to put people back to work and to help local jurisdictions. Bel Air immediately began considering public works needs that would help the community weather this economic crisis, calling a special election on the question of sewerage. Voters approved the proposed new sewer project, which included a nine-mile pipeline, two pumping stations with force mains and a sewage disposal plant south of Bynum Run on Churchville Road at a cost of $110,000. The town hired Mr. J. Spence Howard to design, supervise and construct the sewer and disposal plant and submitted a loan request to the U.S. Public Works Administration to cover construction costs. Actual construction began in 1933. Funds for the project came partially from the federal government and partially from the sale of bonds.

Later that year, the town board secured funds from the Civil Works Board for labor and construction of a five-foot concrete storm drain on Lee Street from Hickory Avenue to Main Street and another storm drain on Broadway by way of Franklin Street to connect to Lee Street. Everything was done by hand, including excavation and concrete mixing. Workers received seventy-five cents per hour and worked thirty hours per week. The Works Progress Administration also gave grants to construct roads, curbs, gutters and sidewalks along Broadway from Main Street to Williams Street, from Broadway to Gordon Street and along Archer Street from Baltimore Pike to Thomas Street. Bel Air was very fortunate to receive this largesse, but one of the most significant projects was the Bel Air Post Office.

Bel Air's post office had several homes on Main Street since its inception in 1836, when the postal system received its initial authorization by an act of Congress. In the 1930s, the federal government announced several locations under consideration for new facilities as part of the government's plan to create jobs and to upgrade needed facilities. The Bel Air Post Office was one of those chosen for the project. In 1934, the post office real estate division invited local property owners to submit proposals for properties in downtown Bel Air. Twenty-seven property owners responded, citing their location, the size of their property and the price. Prices ranged from $1,250 to $17,000. The review board considered an additional site at the corner of South Main and Courtland Streets, the sheriff's house and the jail. Postal inspectors visited all the sites in December 1934 and met with each property owner, determining that the sheriff's house and the jail provided the perfect location. It was in the center of town and the ideal size. There was only one problem: where would funds come from to replace the house and jail? Everyone recognized that the two were very old and in poor condition, but replacement would be expensive and might create a long-term fiscal problem for the county.

Two weeks later, the county commissioners, the Harford County Delegation and Senator Risteau met to discuss whether the cost of a new jail and residence was manageable. Apparently, this turned out to be too expensive because shortly thereafter the postal inspector announced a new site. The Stevenson A. Williams residence at the corner of Main and Gordon Streets met all the requirements and was offered at a cost of $8,500, down from its initial price of $10,000.

The post office received three bids to build the new structure, but all exceeded the allotted amount by at least $10,000. Negotiations occurred at the federal level, securing the necessary funds by using several sources, including Public Works Administration dollars. In July 1936, the post office approved the bid of the Engineering Contracting Corporation of Baltimore for $52,075 and notified Bel Air's postmaster, Glasgow Archer, that the new post office would be completed in 270 days. The fourth assistant postmaster general, Smith W. Purdum, arrived the day of the notice, spending the night at the Kenmore Inn. He announced that the building would be constructed of native stone from Gatch quarries in Calvary and assured citizens that this site was one of the finest in this section of the country. He directed the contractor to save as many trees as possible and to protect the shrubbery during construction.

Work began at once. The contractor demolished the residence immediately and initiated construction of a seventy-one- by seventy-five-foot structure with a high basement, a public lobby and a cupola. Specifications called for very "modern and handsome" fixtures in the new offices. One of the more interesting features of the new building was the observation catwalk. Every square foot of space inside was subject to observation, while it was impossible for an employee to detect that he was under surveillance. An official could enter the building without being seen and enter his private office, from which a ladder leading to the observation gallery was accessible. The inside walls were painted black and contained special glass, furnished by the government and used in the lower units, enabling one to see out while others could not see in.

Specifications were very exacting and required quality throughout. The contractors used a lead-coated copper roof, which was deemed just as durable as earlier lead roofs that lasted several hundred years. The basement had a moisture-proof room for stamp and envelope storage, and a drain surrounded the entire structure. The lobby floor was made from cement and marble chips. To prevent the floor from getting slippery, an abrasive material was added, and zinc strips used to separate the floor squares. This allowed for expansion and contraction of the floor squares. The wainscoting used in the lobby came from Beaver Dam. It was the last of the marble to come from the dam, so the contractor used great care in its placement, since it could not be duplicated. A mural hand painted by Maxwell Simpson provided the final touch.

The post office opened for business on Friday morning, September 10, 1937. In 1961, the U.S. Postal Service expanded and upgraded the building to include air conditioning at a cost of $245,000. By the 1980s, the postal service recognized a need to expand yet again with the tremendous growth in the Bel Air area. Additionally, technological changes required significant upgrades to meet service demands. A new building followed on Blum Court off Gateway Drive, and the county purchased the original building, later deeding it to the Historical Society of Harford County.

The 1930s also had their share of civil rights issues. As an example, in 1936, two black New Yorkers were refused service at a Bel Air restaurant. This led to a demonstration by seventeen busloads of fellow Works

The post office, built as a WPA project in 1937, brought jobs and hope to Bel Air citizens during the Depression years. *Courtesy of the Historical Society of Harford County.*

Progress Administration workers who, although white, felt the injustice strongly. The workers were en route to Washington for a conference. Although the demonstration was peaceful, forty state police armed with machine guns and tear gas arrived and arrested the two blacks.

By 1937, the requests for aid and loss of jobs were in decline, but there were other issues overshadowing the country and the world. The worldwide economy, lack of leadership and destruction from World War I still plagued many areas, leaving a void that would soon be filled by fascist dictators in Italy, Spain and Germany. By the end of the decade, it was obvious to most people that another world war was imminent, and the county and town braced for yet another tragic decade.

ROOSEVELT'S WAR

On December 7, 1941, Japan attacked Pearl Harbor. Still, even after expecting some form of aggression, locals were shocked at the scale of the attack and its proximity to the United States. Local students listened intently as the schools' public address systems broadcast President Roosevelt's speech decrying the "Day that will live in infamy" the day after the bombing. Most older residents experienced an eerie déjà vu moment—once again we must send our boys off to war. Only this time, the war seemed so much closer. German submarines attacked ships along the Atlantic coast. Hawaii, Alaska and California were potentially in the range of Japanese bombers. Unlike the First World War, procedures were in place to activate the Selective Service Act. Home Guard, rationing and civil defense activities could be resurrected from past programs.

As described by Esther Dombrowski in her article "The Homefront," "Never before and never since has the United States been so supportive of a war." People readily accepted rationing, the draft and extended workweeks and anxiously awaited radio broadcasts about the war's progress. Troops routinely moved through Bel Air. For example, on June 3, 1942, the Twenty-ninth Division spent the night at the armory and then moved to bivouac at the fairgrounds with 2,500 men. Another 10,000 men were expected to pass through the county seat in the next weeks, moving from Cape Cod to North Carolina. Soldiers could be seen everywhere. Even the Lee Street fields next to the high school became

A Main Street parade during World War II.

Wartime rationing caused severe backups as cars lined up for the limited gas available to the civilian population.

a parade ground. The draft expanded to include doctors, dentists and clergymen, leaving some communities without any doctor at all.

Local officials quickly established a ration board at the Richfield Service Station on U.S. Route 1 just south of Bel Air. Volunteers, many of them local schoolteachers, issued ration cards. The ration board reduced milk deliveries to every other day and dropped speed limits to forty miles per hour. Over time, tire rationing became necessary, and the board required anyone with more than five tires for one vehicle to turn in the extras. By 1943, the board had banned all pleasure driving, cut gas rations for "A" card holders (those not involved in defense work or agriculture) to twenty-four gallons every four months and forbade all outdoor Christmas lights. Sugar for canning was available, but residents had to apply for a one-time annual allotment. Bel Air High School home economics teachers provided lessons for residents who did not know how to can. Housewives kept cooking fat jars, salvaging grease for future meals or scrap drives. No major appliances were available, and even bicycles were in short supply.

Because of the shortage of copper, people were asked to turn in pennies for war stamps. Telephone employees actually turned in 10,300 coins at one time. Every week, the county sent out a call for scrap. Bel Air High School held a "tin can day." Thousands of flattened cans poured in. Scrap drives included metal, rubber, newspaper, grease and rags. One reason for the shortages was that it took ten thousand pounds of aluminum to manufacture one fighter plane.

The National Guard Armory in Bel Air served as the Civilian Defense Headquarters, with all messages and plans for county units organized there. Men not eligible for military service because of age, deferment or essential defense work joined the Home Guard, training at the American Legion for guard duty, riot control, first aid and evacuation procedures. Because few weapons were available, the county asked citizens to donate 1903 Springfield or 1917 Enfield rifles for the Home Guard's use. Bel Air units, under Wakeman Munnikhuysen, John Worthington III and T. Roy Brookes, included sixty-six men.

New defense plants and factories appeared as if overnight, bringing defense workers from across the country to Bel Air and the surrounding communities. The Glenn L. Martin Company in Baltimore County and the War Department paid for instructors and materials at Bel Air High School and other county schools to help train workers for the specialized needs of area factories. Classes ran day and night. Shortages of gasoline and rubber forced the use of public transportation. A new "War Time Zone" was added to Standard and Daylight Savings in an effort to conserve heat and light. Defense workers soon complained of exorbitant rents, so a governmental agency stepped in, rolling back rents to levels from April 1941 and requiring landlords to register every local rental property at Bel Air High School. Again, teachers volunteered to man the registration office and ensure fair rates.

With so many men serving, workers were in short supply, so wages and high overtime pay became the norm. Women came forward to fill many of these positions, entering careers never considered before—like loading shells, handling explosives and testing guns. The Red Cross organized women all over the county to meet in small groups to sew and knit for the British War Relief and, later, the American military. Ladies were advised to bring sandwiches and stay all day. Just as in World War I, the Gray Ladies and Red Cross volunteers like Josephine Dallam, Violet MacLean and Caroline Hopkins took first aid courses, attended classes to learn how to make surgical dressings, led blood drives, assisted wounded soldiers, organized "bandage rollers" and provided food and entertainment for the troops and then organized other local women to assist.

Children also helped with the war effort in numerous ways, buying bonds, acting as bike messengers and plane spotters and practicing for potential fire bombings with the sand buckets ever present in school hallways. They memorized card photos of every potential type of aircraft and spent hours on hills around town watching for enemy planes. A telephone installed at each spotting station provided a means to call in any plane spotted, whether friend or foe. The spotter reported the number of planes, the number of motors on each, the distance from the ground (high or low), the station code name, the direction the planes came from and the direction from the station where the planes were headed. All of this information was forwarded immediately to the Baltimore Center, where the information was tallied and reconciled with other reports.

Every student received a book to purchase war stamps. Stamps cost $0.10 apiece. When you reached $18.75, you received a $25.00 war bond. The big push was not the savings but helping to win the war, and it didn't hurt that students who participated could ride in army vehicles— jeeps, trucks and the like— that were brought to the schools to encourage purchases. Incentives to buy war bonds were not confined to schools. The Argonne Movie Theater regularly held "War Bond Matinees." Admission required purchase of a war bond. The bonds were also available at banks, post offices, festivals and special events.

Local governments adjusted rules to meet the war needs as well. Farms needed manpower during harvest, and most of the young men were off at war, so prisoners from Aberdeen Proving Ground and Edgewood Arsenal became the new farmworkers. The problem was transportation. It became routine for young boys of fourteen or so to drive trucks, transporting prisoners from Aberdeen Proving Ground and Edgewood Arsenal Prisons to area farms and produce to markets in Baltimore. The prisoners were accompanied by one or two soldiers, who acted as guards. Stories abounded about German and Italian prisoners working the dairy farms and picking tomatoes, corn and beans at local farms. Most of the German prisoners worked hard, doing whatever was required, but they did not interact with the locals. They generally returned home after the war, although some kept in touch with their farm employers. In one instance, east of Bel Air, a German doctor who worked on a farm on Thomas Run Road returned several years later with his family. The farmer opened the door to a knock on Christmas Eve to find the man who had become a good friend during the war and through correspondence afterward. The doctor and his family eventually became American citizens. Many of the Italians stayed after the war, having made friends here, particularly among the Italian-American community.

Many lessons from World War I helped mobilization efforts. There were no longer sprawling camps but smaller training fields to avoid earlier health issues. Once units were federalized, many of the guardsmen from Bel Air used Baltimore's Montgomery Ward building as headquarters and trained in nearby Carroll Park. Others trained at converted beach hotels, golf courses and similar facilities—anywhere the government could provide training facilities and pistol ranges.

There were many challenges. Equipment was more sophisticated than in previous times. For example, the new B-29s, still in the experimental stage, contained computerized equipment never before seen by most airmen. Bob Marzicola, a local airman, described learning how to operate the new computer-operated gunnery and the bombing radar. The planes were so new that training took place over fields in Kansas and Nebraska to allow time and space to correct problems like overheating engines and a host of maladies yet to be discovered.

Young men, anxious to be part of the action, got their mothers to give permission for them to sign up at only seventeen. Local boys soon shipped out for Europe and the Pacific. One local soldier told of meeting three other servicemen in Saipan in the midst of the war. All were Bel Air High School graduates. Bel Air men served the nation proudly throughout the conflict. Some, like Lieutenant General Milton A. Reckord, went down in history for their tremendous contributions in Europe. Others served in nonmilitary roles but provided equally important contributions. Russell and Kate Lord, who went on to produce a national magazine, *The Land*, after the war, worked closely with the Roosevelt Administration in several positions. Kate worked for a clandestine branch of the Weather Bureau, using her artistic abilities to draw technical maps for Allied pilots conducting bombing raids over enemy territory. Russell worked with the Treasury Department, writing and designing pamphlets and posters seeking to boost war bond sales to farmers. His work with the farming community on conservation led to an invitation from the British Ministry of Agriculture to lend his expertise to the war-ravaged country as a representative of the United States Office of War Information. He traveled throughout England for two months, speaking with people and assessing damages and probable postwar consequences for England's agricultural industry.

Finally, on May 7, 1945, the war in Europe ended, and in August, the Japanese surrendered. The exaltation was short-lived as reality set in. Long unemployment lines formed as veterans returned home, and the scale of the loss of lives became obvious. The physical and emotional toll was heavy indeed. Yet peace lasted only a few years.

Truman's War and Beyond

In June 1950, war broke out between the Republic of Korea and the Democratic People's Republic of Korea. The war was primarily the result of the political division of Korea after World War II. Japan ruled Korea from 1910 to 1945. Following Japan's surrender, American administrators divided the peninsula along the Thirty-eighth Parallel, with U.S. forces occupying the south and Soviet forces occupying the north. Within five years, civil war broke out, leading to the first conflict of the Cold War, placing the southern democratic regime directly against the communist regime. Again, Bel Air men and boys were called to war. This time, the country failed to rally at the level of the previous war. Perhaps the deprivation of the previous years had worn down the community's resolve; perhaps Korea just seemed so far away and insubstantial, or perhaps it was a simple case of fatigue. Still, many were called to serve, and many died or were injured.

By 1950, the draft impacted twenty to thirty young men per month. By the following year, reports of local men dying in Korea had become too frequent, and losses continued unabated until the fighting stopped in 1953. At home, the first air raid drills to deal with potential nuclear attacks began, using sirens from area firehouses as warning signals. These soldiers came home to a very different Bel Air and a very different country. The Cold War years took their toll. By the late 1960s and the outbreak of the Vietnam War, the country faced the long-term impacts of the assassination of President Kennedy, the civil rights era, the coming of age of the baby boom generation and the political discontent of a nation weary of wars. Bel Air dealt with the changes in a somewhat more restrained manner. The armory remained the center of community activities. The Aberdeen Proving Ground continued to provide a strong employment base, and people went about their daily lives much as they always had. But change was inevitable, and change came.

VI

SUBURBIA AND THE
MEGALOPOLIS

TRACT HOUSING AND THE BABY BOOM

With the end of World War II, a housing crisis brewed as many soldiers and defense workers decided to remain in Bel Air to start families. The GI Bill offered new possibilities for education and opened up unprecedented professional options. Many former farmers decided to take advantage of this once-in-a-lifetime opportunity. Simultaneously, technological advances, many of these the result of wartime experiments, led to mechanization and consolidation of area farms, leaving small farm operations in the lurch. The dairy industry, always one of the county's mainstays, was particularly hard hit, with declining prices, increasing costs and regulations and the effects of large corporate operations.

One of the first to recognize the demand for new housing options and to take advantage of the potential for land development was Friederick (Fritz) Kelly and his wife, Margaret, the owners of Liriodendron. They formed the Bel Air Company and worked with local contractors to develop Bel Air's first postwar subdivision, thus eliminating the farmland southwest of town. The new development, known as Howard Park after Mr. Kelly's father, Howard Atwood Kelly, began construction in 1951 and included small ranchers. Some of the later houses were prefabricated based on a new technology developed by the National Development Corporation. Houses were inexpensive and required very little money down due to the GI Bill. Sales were brisk, and local farmers began to see

Dr. Howard Kelly, one of the "Big Four" at Johns Hopkins Hospital, built Liriodendron in 1897 as a summer home for his wife, Laetitia Bredow Kelly, to combat her homesickness for Prussia. *Courtesy of the Historical Society of Harford County.*

the potential for financial gain. Within a short time, similar developments were planned south of Bel Air.

With the influx of new families, students quickly outpaced capacity, and a new high school opened in 1950 on what was once Kenmore Farm, adding the twelfth grade now required by state law and eliminating another farm. Under the tutelage of coach Al Cesky, Bel Air High School soon became a major football school. Until then, only Havre de Grace High School had a football team. For the first time, boys who did not come from a farming background made up the majority of the school's enrollment, allowing more time for sports. Equipping the team was still a hurdle, but on November 1, 1950, they played the first intramural game with Havre de Grace. Before long, these games became so popular that crowds of 2,500 or more gathered on Friday nights for all home games. Afterward, many of the kids headed for Reuben's Drive Inn (the old Del Haven site) to experience yet another innovation of the times—a drive-in restaurant with roller-skating waitresses and shakes, fries and burgers. This became the place to see and be seen for the local high school crowd.

Suburbia and the Megalopolis

After the war, many of the scientists and professionals at Aberdeen Proving Ground and Edgewood Arsenal remained in Bel Air. They placed major emphasis on education for their children and became very active in the local PTAs. Local teachers emphasized ever greater academic achievement, organizing the Bel Air Forum, which brought guest speakers to Bel Air, including such luminaries as Captain Hyman Rickover, Reverend Norman Vincent Peale, author William Shirer, Senator William Fulbright and even British foreign policy leader Clement Atlee.

Smaller farms north of town also began to disappear to development. By the 1960s, the county needed several new schools, a new hospital, new government services, new equipment and new town and county offices. The courthouse could no longer service the needs of this burgeoning population, which almost doubled in just one decade. Over the next few years, the town built a new administration building with its own police facilities and added a public works building in 1973 to house offices and equipment. Simultaneously, the county built a new Health Department on Hays Street (demolished in 2010), the Bel Air Library (expanded twice since then), a new firehouse (again expanded significantly in the last two decades) and, in 1961, a new county office building to house the county government offices and a modern jail at 45 South Main Street.

According to a description in the 1961 minutes of the Institute of Maryland Public Affairs, the jail, managed by the county sheriff, Raymond Fulker, had an anteroom with several filing cabinets. Seventeen of the cabinet drawers contained firearm permits, and one drawer contained stolen gun reports. There was a single desk and a barred window through which visitors could talk to inmates during visiting hours. A radio room linked the sheriff's office with five radio-controlled cars and held a display of wanted criminals dating back to 1946. Toward the back of the room was a heavy door leading to the cells. The first floor contained a kitchen and dining hall. Trustees carried trays to the individual cells. There were three cells per floor, holding four prisoners each. The cells contained four bunks, necessary plumbing and one light enclosed by shatterproof glass. The second floor contained two cells for women with enclosed showers and better lighting and one cell for juveniles. The third floor had one cell for Negro prisoners, and the lowest floor had a "drunk tank" for prisoners to sober up. In all, the jail could hold twenty prisoners at a time, an acceptable capacity in 1961.

Within a short time, the jail could no longer meet county needs, so in 1969, the county built a modern prison on the town's former dumpsite, in what was known as Frogtown. The new $1.4 million prison opened in 1973 and was expanded yet again in 2011. The county also closed the almshouse in the '60s, dividing the property into several parcels, including the Equestrian Center, Heavenly Waters Park and a new dumpsite, known as Tollgate Landfill.

In 1956, night classes for the newly organized Harford Community College started at Bel Air High School. New junior high schools and new elementary schools soon followed. With so many new residents and new buildings, accompanied by a severe drought, the Bel Air Water Company ran dry in the summer of 1954. The state authorized an emergency tap of Winters Run, but a long-term solution became critical, and the company's well system was abandoned, shifting to Winters Run as its primary water source. Once the town and the company resolved the water issue, albeit temporarily, development began again.

In 1961, developers submitted proposals to expand Howard Park, and town commissioners decided it was time to update zoning and subdivision regulations. Pressure was on to expand development along Rockspring Avenue, Broadway and Hickory Avenue, as well as the traditional areas of Main and Bond Streets. For a time, this was seen as progress. Large old homes and the farms surrounding Bel Air began disappearing regularly. First, the Worthington farm became Homestead Village, and then the Durham farm on Route 1 became Kunkels, International Harvester and the Central Motors Company. Next, the Baltimore Archdiocese purchased the Wagner farm next to the sewer-pumping station and Homestead Village for a new parochial high school for 1,200 students and a 40-person staff. Acre after acre changed hands, and bulldozers dotted the countryside. By 1963, development pressures had reached the northeast part of town, and apartment development started with 42 units on Crocker Street and 119 units on Moores Mill Road. This was a new phenomenon for Bel Air, at first seen as luxury living.

With all of the new residents, retail had to follow. In 1963, surveyors from Frederick Ward and Associates began plans for Bel Air Plaza. Initially, some businesses expressed concern about competition, but several stores saw this as an opportunity to become part of the new trend of car-oriented retailing and started negotiations with the Julio family, owners of the shopping center. Then, in 1964, the state legislature eliminated racing dates at all half-mile tracks, essentially closing any future activities at the Bel Air Racetrack. The track owner, working with Bel Air's mayor, decided to request annexation of the property for use as an industrial park. Meanwhile, local businessmen started organizing several development projects in and around town. Some, such as the Shamrock Nursing Home, succeeded, while others, like the Worthington Village Shopping Center, fell flat. The plan for development of this three-hundred-acre farm south of Bel Air was eventually downscaled, resulting in the Country Village Apartments and Bradford Village, Bel Air's only planned unit development.

The farms were not the only casualties. Bel Air, once the home of numerous inns and Victorian residences, began losing these treasures one by one. Safeway purchased the Kenmore Inn and the adjoining Hays House. It worked with the community to move a portion of the historic Hays House but demolished the inn for the new supermarket. The old Circle Inn on Main Street met a similar fate as Acme built a new, larger, more modern supermarket next to the post office.

By this time, local residents had decided enough was enough and filed a suit known as *Beshore v. Town of Bel Air* in an attempt to stop Bel Air Plaza. The suit failed, and development continued, with Bel Air noted as one of the four fastest-growing areas in the Baltimore region in 1965.

The town grew by 86 percent between 1960 and 1970, and 40 percent of that new growth was due to apartment development designed for younger and older couples. By the 1970s, development issues could no longer be ignored in the town or the surrounding county. Water and sewer services could not keep pace with demand. Traffic congestion grew every day. Main Street resembled a ghost town, reflecting the move of area businesses to the shopping centers lining Route 1 and the problems created by a botched project to improve the Main Street streetscape in 1980. The development downturn in the early 1980s was actually a mixed blessing. It bought some time for the town and county to resolve some of their infrastructure issues by building a new county water treatment facility and the Sod Run Sewer Treatment Plant. The town's water system expanded to include a new water tower and necessary capacity improvements. The roadways were even more problematic. The State Highway Administration introduced new one-way traffic systems and built a new expressway, Route 24, connecting I-95 and the Bel Air Bypass. But traffic continued to worsen as more and more people moved into the county's designated growth areas north and south of town, virtually eliminating most of the farms between Bel Air and the coastal area to the south.

Bel Air's rural days faded, succumbing to the inevitable suburbanization dictated by its location in the megalopolis between Boston and Washington, D.C. Still, all is not gloom and doom. The core of the town remains very strong. Small shops once again line Main Street; while these are not the hardware and general stores of earlier years, the restaurants and specialty stores provide a comfortable, cheerful gathering place. Merchants, residents and officials work together to bring people downtown. They may not be coming for farm supplies on Friday nights as in the days of old, but they come for the festivals, outdoor movies, art shows and shopping experiences. The Farmers' Market, established in 1976, draws people from the entire county on Tuesdays and Saturdays. Parades and concerts entertain residents regularly, and the armory remains a gathering place and community center.

TECHNOLOGY—BEAUTY OR THE BEAST

The coming of hard-surfaced roads and reliable automobiles and trucks led the way for many changes. Initially, the new mobility helped the farmers, making it easier and more efficient for them to get their products to outlying markets. Over time, the reverse movement of new suburban residents made the agricultural economy less and less viable. Land prices skyrocketed. The agricultural support services essential to retaining a critical mass of farms began to lose ground. Eventually, this led to a shift from a farm economy to a service and technology economy with all of the turmoil that major change produces. The needs of newer, faster automobiles and the ever-increasing suburbanites led to the development of new major highways. Bel Air soon became a "bedroom" community with workers commuting to Baltimore and even Washington, D.C. So, while acclimating to such new gadgets and innovations as electric typewriters, dial telephones and zip codes, residents now dealt with the Bel Air Bypass, Interstate 95 and Maryland Route 24—high-speed, limited-access highways bringing noise, traffic and more new residents. Along with these "improvements" came a major new industry. The housing boom needed developers and engineers to prepare the surveys and plans and contractors to actually construct these new buildings. Bel Air became the home of engineering firms like Frederick Ward Associates, Morris Ritchie Associates, G.W. Stephens & Associates and many others that helped develop the plans and change the landscape of the entire county.

The Ward family, early pioneers in the local development industry, led the way in the shifting economic focus. The family came to the area in 1930 as part of the out migration from Appalachia, or more specifically from Watauga, North Carolina. Many families from the North Carolina hill country relocated as the once fertile soils and forests were depleted and the Depression years took their toll on the area. Walter Lucky Ward, his wife and seven children, heavily impacted by the hardships of the Depression and the limited opportunities at home, decided to join this peregrination, finding themselves a place in Fallston, Maryland, as tenant farmers on the Scarff farm near Upper Cross Roads. Between 1930 and 1940, the family moved several times, farming at Rock Run, the Mahoney farm in Bel Air (the original Booth family farm, which was known as Tudor Hall) and the Skillman farm on Winters Run. In 1940, Mr. Ward decided to leave farming for building and carpentry. This was true of many of the North Carolina migrants who found jobs at Aberdeen Proving Grounds and Edgewood Arsenal with better pay and better working conditions.

The family moved to Bel Air in 1944 and thus began a development dynasty. One of the sons, R. Walter Ward, started his own construction company with his longtime friend Melvin Bosley in 1950. Their first project was Howard Park, transforming the Kelly family orchards into tract housing to meet the needs of the postwar housing boom. From there, they bought farms throughout the area and led the way in new suburban development. Another son, Fred Ward, went on to the University of Maryland. Upon graduating, he started Frederick Ward Associates, a land-surveying firm that still operates as an engineering, surveying and land-planning firm on Main Street in Bel Air, although it is now owned by Fred's son Craig. Other developers and engineering firms soon followed as the development surrounding Bel Air mushroomed.

With all of the postwar development, commercial expansion was inevitable, at first along Main Street and later along Route 1. One of the more enterprising projects began in 1946, when Charles L. Lutz, a local entrepreneur, purchased three houses along North Main Street running from Pennsylvania Avenue (then known as Greene Street) to the Methodist Episcopal Church. Ms. Millicent Young owned the corner property, and the remaining land and dwellings were owned jointly by Florence Maulsby, Roberta Hollingsworth and Elizabeth and Minnie Smithers. Mr. Lutz explained that he hoped "to build modern stores as soon as building conditions permit." Groundbreaking occurred in September 1946, with completion of his new store in August 1947. The *Aegis* reported that two thousand persons visited the new store even before the grand opening. The article described the new structure, "from the red and black plastic façade with its ornamental neon signs to the rear entrance and indoor landing platform, the three story concrete block building is modern in every detail—streamlined for efficient utility." The article went on to explain that the building is fitted with "such streamlined refinements as a PBX switchboard complete with inter-store communications, a freight elevator and the latest type of neon indirect lighting." There was a parts department in the basement and a twenty-person service department. According to the *Aegis* reports of August 15, 1947, the grand opening was "a huge success, with an estimated crowd of between five and six thousand." The new store carried bathroom fixtures, kitchen appliances, electronics and commercial refrigeration equipment, but the major interest came from the advent of consumer electronics, televisions and air conditioners.

Lutz was the consummate marketing genius. He advertised that the store was a primary dealership for GE televisions packaged in handsome cabinets veneered with genuine Honduran mahogany, touting the big pictures on the ten-inch direct view tube. He installed "a super colossal receiver" in the American Legion Post #39 that was used for nightly reception of sports events and routinely invited the public to the store to watch popular events and programs, such as the Monday night fights. One of these was the Joe Louis Exhibition Bout held on February 9, 1948. To put this in perspective, in 1946, only eight thousand American households had televisions; by 1960, a mere fourteen years later, 47.5 million households across the country had televisions. Lutz was a true visionary, seeing the potential not only for the television but also for other mass-produced appliances like washing machines, vacuum cleaners and refrigerators. These were unavailable during the war years, so there was pent-up demand, and they were cheap enough that most families could afford them, particularly with the installment plans offered by the Appliance Store.

One of the most popular products was the air conditioner. A 1950 *Newsweek* headline, "Air Conditioning: Booming Like Television," reported that "the nation's electric power usage jumped three percent in just two weeks in June as homeowners all over the country turned on their new air conditioners." Lutz Appliance Store carried Frigidaire room air conditioners for $389.50, advertising that a customer could purchase a "completely self contained air conditioning unit...simply plug it in and adjust controls for desired results." Lutz soon expanded his holdings, leasing his adjoining store on Main Street to Bata Shoe and leasing a new unit on Pennsylvania Avenue for a barbershop. Residential units along this portion of North Main Street soon disappeared to commercial ventures. Then, in the late '60s, the shopping centers began to pull commercial ventures away from Main Street and a new type of retail dawned.

Within a few years, Harford Mall and Tollgate Marketplace joined Bel Air Plaza, creating a shopping mecca for the new residents in the suburban communities surrounding Bel Air. Many new stores came to the town with these developments, and many others moved away from the old commercial areas on Main Street. The new centers provided large movie complexes, eventually replacing the old Bel Air Movie Theater and then being replaced themselves by even larger complexes south of town. Perhaps the most distressing development for locals was the loss of Bessie the cow. For many years, one farm held out against the development pressures along Route 1; then Glen Deaton, the property owner, died, and the land was sold. There was great concern about Bessie's future, but arrangements were made for her to spend her remaining days at a local farm in Forest Hill. In 2000, the Bel Air Town Center completed the quad of shopping centers at the intersection of Route 1 and Route 24.

The Harford Mall opened in 1972, six years after the Bel Air Racetrack closed, but many memories of the track endured for locals. The new Korvettes and Montgomery Ward and the expanded Woolworths and cafeteria were widely acclaimed, but nostalgia made the occasion a mixed blessing. Len Chapel, who sold *News American* newspapers at the track as a child in the 1950s, wrote with fondness of his days at the track competing with the other "sellers," the fried chicken sold on Tollgate Road, the races and the annual county fair. Others told of WBAL radio personality Galen Fromm bringing Happy Johnny and his Hillbilly Gang to sing "You Are My Sunshine" to open the fair. With each new center, competition heightened for downtown stores. Some, like Peppi's Meat Market, offered unique products that brought clients from across the state for their specialized German fare that could not be found in large grocery stores, something hard to find in any store.

Joseph "Peppi" Simmeth immigrated to the states after World War II and became a fixture in the community. He worked in his family's butcher shop in Germany and was the fourth generation to follow in the meat-making business. In 1956, he moved to New York City, where he worked for three years before moving to Harford County to work at Benson's Meat Market. Ten years later, he and his wife opened a store on Hays Street across from the final site. They worked together cooking and selling their unique products. She told the story that while pregnant with her third child, Peppi would tell her they couldn't afford to have a child except on a Sunday. She had to work in the store the rest of the week. Sure enough, after finishing work on Saturday night, she woke at 6:00 a.m. on Sunday morning and told Peppi it was time to go to the hospital. When he retired in 1988, his employee David Moser and his wife purchased the store and operated it using the same special recipes until the land was purchased by the county in 2009.

This proved true for many of the old stores that remained downtown; those with specialties and long-term clientele like Harrison's Paints, Bel Air Bakery and Boyd and Fulford Drugstore continued to do well.

The next major development occurred on Route 24, with the Upper Chesapeake Medical Center. Until this time, county residents were served by Fallston General Hospital and Harford Memorial Hospital in Havre de Grace. Both facilities were outdated and had numerous issues. In the 1980s, the town annexed land along the newly completed highway, originally planning development of a hotel, since the town no longer had any overnight accommodations. This was not to be. Owners of the land approached the town with a plan to build a hospital complex that would replace the existing aging facilities in Fallston and provide a major employer for the Bel Air area. Since its initial development, the facility has expanded several times and is currently in the throes of yet another expansion for a much-needed cancer center. The medical center is now the town's largest employer and has outpaced all projections for patient care.

During the twentieth century, the town experienced several cataclysmic occurrences. The defense plants and military complex so necessary during World War II continued to thrive after the war years, bringing jobs and residents to the area. Glenn L. Martin's was one of these major employers. On December 9, 1953, an experimental jet plane carrying a pilot and copilot from the Middle River plant exploded in midair a mile above Bel Air. The wreckage spread for miles around what is now John Carroll High School. The plane's fuselage was projected over John D. Worthington's property, the Homestead, and landed on Dr. M. Wagner's farm. Although the pilot and copilot were able to eject from the plane, one man died and the other was seriously injured. A commercial airliner flying over the scene at the time circled the wreckage until military officials arrived. The Bel Air Volunteer Fire Department responded, citing this as one of the most spectacular and dangerous incidents in Bel Air's history because of the proximity to homes and the real danger of fire from the jet fuel.

In 1972, disaster struck again, this time in the form of a major fire. Main Street was not a stranger to fires, but the worst of these blazes occurred on Groundhog Day 1972. The inferno destroyed six businesses: the Vaughn Hotel, the American Store, the local bowling alley, Preston's Stationery, the Hole (a restaurant) and Mike Smithson's barbershop. It left several apartment dwellers homeless. The fire started when a fuel tank overflowed while being filled and was subsequently ignited by a gas water heater. The fire raged for four hours and caused $2 million in damages. The buildings were eventually replaced by the Red Fox Restaurant, which is now the Tower Restaurant. The apartments no longer exist.

With all of the development and the influx of new residents, the social and cultural makeup of the community also underwent a metamorphosis.

SOCIAL AND CULTURAL EVOLUTION

With the changing development patterns, more leisure time brought a demand for new parks, golf courses and cultural activities. By the 1950s, the baby boomers became a market unto themselves, which quickly changed the area landscape. The Bel Air Roller Rink opened on Route 1, and a bowling alley followed just south of Bel Air. Soon, sports complexes of all types spread throughout the county. There were now several theater groups, a cultural center and a museum at the Liriodendron, the former Kelly home, and a rail-to-trail project along the former Ma & Pa Railroad bed. One of the more creative efforts was the opening of the Bel Air Opera in 1961. The opera opened in 1963 as a summer theater offering a summer season of five major productions starring both local artists and those from across the country. The artists enjoyed a summer in a charming country location and rave reviews from critics in Baltimore, Washington and Bel Air. Saul Lilienstein was the artistic director and conductor, providing a wide range of operas in English, making them both entertaining and accessible. The Opera Company was strongly supported by many local luminaries.

Saul Lilienstein, an internationally recognized conductor, was the artistic director for the Harford Opera Theater for several years, bringing nationally known talent to Bel Air each summer from such places as Baltimore, New York and San Francisco. *Courtesy of the Historical Society of Harford County.*

The company originally met in a 125-year-old barn on the grounds of Harford Community College, a building that was later condemned. Seats came from the now-defunct racetrack. Like any new venture, the company was fraught with problems in the beginning; one of the more interesting occurred just before opening night. The performers practicing late into the night were stopped by a farmer, who threatened the company with a shotgun if they didn't shut up. The next night, the farmer drew up on his tractor running it at full throttle to disrupt the performance. After some discussion, a solution was found, and the opera went on, but at its end the rains came. The dirt roads and parking lot filled up with mud, and some cars were mired for days. Still, the enthusiasm for the opera did not wane, and the group went on for another twenty years.

In 1976, the Bel Air Farmers' Market opened on Hickory Avenue. Planners hoped to bring shoppers back to the downtown area and to provide farmers with a new market. The market continues to grow today and is cherished by longtime residents as a meeting place, as well as a source of fresh fruits and vegetables, music and art.

After World War II, social changes in the role of women became inevitable, although these were slow and sometimes torturous. Mary Risteau broke the male barrier to become the first woman to serve in the Maryland House of Delegates. She went on to become a state senator and a beloved representative of the community. Eventually, the Board of Education eliminated its ruling that married women could not teach, and in the 1980s, June Weeks served as chair of the Bel Air Town Board. Barriers were coming down, but civil rights issues played a large role throughout the country during the 1960s and '70s. The Harford County Board of Education refused to integrate schools for many years, causing much bitterness and frustration. Finally, bending to federal requirements, integration of all Harford County schools became a reality in 1965–66. The Ku Klux Klan continued to have rallies in and around Bel Air throughout the '60s. In one instance, robed KKK members sauntered down Bond Street after their meeting was canceled in Forest Hill due to threats of arrests.

The most scandalous incident occurred in 1970 at the height of the national civil rights movement. Ralph Featherstone, a thirty-one-year-old black man and former organizer of the Student Nonviolent Coordinating Committee, and his associate William Che Payne died when a bomb they were carrying exploded prematurely, destroying the tollhouse on Bel Air Road at Tollgate Road. According to state police reports, they were carrying explosives on their way to a pretrial hearing for their friend H. Rap Brown, a Black Panther leader who was charged with inciting a race riot in Cambridge, Maryland, in 1967. Brown embodied the new, aggressive black nationalism of the 1960s. He wore a signature black leather jacket, black beret, dark glasses and full-blown Afro. He spoke out against racism and supported the idea that rebellion—violent if necessary—was acceptable. Because of the explosion and the subsequent highly publicized comments of the judge concerning the defendant, the trial was moved to Ellicott City, Maryland. Brown failed to show for the April trial date but was arrested in October 1971 in Manhattan, where he was involved in a robbery and bar shootout, wounding two city police officers.

The racial tensions of the time are hard to exaggerate, but Bel Air fared better than most. Although slow to recognize the injustices of the past, changes began to occur. In 1966, Godfrey Herman Clayton became the county's first black parole and probation officer. Others soon followed in government and white-collar positions. Lifestyles and mindsets were changing.

Bel Air Today

By 2012, the visible boundary of farms separating the town and county disappeared, replaced by suburbia. The Town of Bel Air includes three square miles of land and 10,211 people, but the Greater Bel Air area, beyond the incorporated boundaries, boasts a population of 58,568 in a county of 249,753 people. The hospital and government remain the major employers, and the military continues to play a major role in employment and local life, having added eight thousand jobs at Aberdeen Proving Grounds in the last five years with the BRAC initiative. Today, there are more people, houses, jobs, schools, parks, ballfields, shops, cars and money than in the past, but this is tempered by less time and tolerance and fewer woods, farms and meadows.

Route 1, the historic major gateway to Bel Air and its Main Street, once a major north–south corridor along the eastern seaboard, provides primary access to the town's commercial hub. Interstate traffic primarily uses I-95; still, traffic congestion along Bel Air's roadways remains both a curse and a blessing, stressing drivers while bringing needed customers to area stores and activities. Bel Air now hosts banks from across the country and beyond. Its streets are lined with restaurants, shops, service businesses and government offices laced with pocket parks and enhanced with gardens and well-kept structures. Perhaps the town's greatest achievement is its retention of a sense of community and an appreciation of its rich heritage, which is highlighted by its many community events, festivals and partnerships with local businesses and residents.

BIBLIOGRAPHY

BOOKS

Arnold, Joseph, and Anirban Basu. *Maryland Old Line to New Prosperity.* Sun Valley, CA: American History Press, 2003.

Bailyn, Bernard. *Voyagers to the West: A Passage in the Peopling of America on the Eve of the American Revolution.* New York: Vintage Books, 1986.

Bibbins, Mrs. Arthur Barnevila. *The Beginnings of Maryland in England/ America.* Baltimore, MD: Remington Company, 1934.

Bruger, Robert J. *Maryland: A Middle Temperament, 1634–1980.* Baltimore, MD: Johns Hopkins University Press, 1988.

Carr, Lois Green, Russell R. Menard and Lorena S. Walsh. *Robert Cole's World: Agriculture and Society in Early Maryland.* Chapel Hill: University of North Carolina Press, 1991.

Chrismer, James E. *From Mustard Seed to Tree of Life: A Centennial History of St. Margaret Parish, Bel Air, Maryland 1905–2005.* N.p., 2005.

Harford County Directory. Baltimore, MD: State Directories Publishing Company, 1953.

Hawke, David F., and Richard Balkin, eds. *Everyday Life in Early America.* New York: Harper & Row, 1988.

Kruger, Mollee. *The Cobbler's Last.* Rockville, MD: Maryben Books, 2010.

Larew, Marilynn M. *Bel Air: An Architectural and Cultural History, 1782–1945.* Edited by Carol L. Deibel and Elizabeth M. Carven. Annapolis, MD: Fishergate, Inc., 1995.

———. *Bel Air: The Town through Its Buildings.* Edited by Christopher Weeks. Edgewood, MD: Northfield Press Inc., 1981.

Noyes, Terry A. *History of the Harford County Sheriff's Office.* Nashville, TN: Turner Publishing Company, 2006.

Preston, Walter W. *History of Harford County, Maryland, 1608–1812.* Baltimore, MD: Genealogical Publishing Co., 1990.

Sanborn Map Company. *Bel Air: Harford County, MD, February 1904.* New York: Sanborn Map Company, 1910.

Scharf, J. Thomas. *History of Maryland from the Earliest Period to the Present Day.* Hatboro, PA: Tradition Press, 1967.

Tucker, Barclay E. *Bel Air Centennial Committee, Inc. Commemorative Book: 1874–1974.* Town of Bel Air, MD, 1974.

Titone, Nora. *My Thoughts Be Bloody.* New York: Free Press, 2010.

Weeks, Christopher. *An Architectural History of Harford County, Maryland.* Baltimore, MD: Johns Hopkins University Press, 1996.

Wright, C. Milton. *Our Harford Heritage: A History of Harford County, Maryland.* 3rd ed. Glen Burnie, MD: French-Bray Printing Company, 1980.

BULLETINS

Bowers, Deborah Jean. "A One-Hundred Year History of Libraries in Harford County from 1885." *Harford Historical Bulletin* 67 (1996).

Chrismer, James E. "Russell and Kate Lord: Harford's Artist of the Land." *Harford Historical Bulletin* 106 (2007).

Corddry, Mary Umbarger. "Forever the Land: The Legacy of Russell and Kate Lord." *Harford Historical Bulletin* 106 (2007).

Craig, David R. "History of the Havre de Grace Racetrack." *Harford Historical Bulletin* 59 (1994).

Dombrowski, Esther. "The Homefront: Harford County During World War II." *Harford Historical Bulletin* 65 (1995).

———. "The Homefront: Harford County During World War II, Part II." *Harford Historical Bulletin* 66 (1995).

Jones, John H. "Harford County and World War I: the Military Heritage." *Harford Historical Bulletin* 109 (2010).

Liedlich, Fred. "History of Susquehanna Baseball League, 1946–1953—Part I." *Harford Historical Bulletin* 90 (2001).

Washburn, Douglas. "The Colored Schools of Harford County: Separate and Equal?" *Harford Historical Bulletin* 102 (2006).

Wooddell, Paul J. "Harford's Greatest Generation: World War II Remembrances of Harford Citizens." *Harford Historical Bulletin* 87 (2001).

Manuscripts and Interviews

Cameron, Broadnax, Sr. Oral History Interview with James Massey, January 1975. Harford County Public Library. Bel Air, MD.

Cassilly, Nancy Webster. Interview by author, March 2012. Bel Air, MD.

Cook, Richard, DVM. Interview by author, March 2012. Bel Air, MD.

Dombrowski, Esther. Oral History Interview with Douglas Washburn, June 17, 2003. Harford County Public Library. Bel Air, MD.

Getz, Payson. Oral History Interview with Douglas Washburn, June 20, 2002. Harford County Public Library. Bel Air, MD.

Hall, Mary. Oral History Interview with James Massey, June 17, 1980. Harford County Public Library. Bel Air, MD.

Kelly, Fritz H. Oral History Interview with Jenny Foster, August 11, 1971. Bel Air, MD.

Linebaugh, Donald W. *Lutz Building: Maryland Historical Trust Maryland Inventory of Historic Properties.* Crownsville: Maryland Historical Trust, 2009.

Moore, Hannah. Oral History Interview with Celestia Simmons, March 23, 1981. Harford County Public Library. Bel Air, MD.

Reedy, Orley G. Oral History Interview with Marie Johnson, April 1980. Harford County Public Library. Bel Air, MD.

Robbins, Charles L. "One Man's Journey: An Oral History Interview with Charles L. Robbins." Interview by author, November 2011. Bel Air, MD.

Van Bibber, George. *Notes on Bel Air: A Character Study of Our County Seat.* Bel Air, MD: Historical Society of Harford County, Inc., n.d.

———. Oral History Interview, June 1972. Harford County Public Library. Bel Air, MD.

Ward, R. Walter. Oral History Interview, March 16, 2001. Harford County Public Library. Bel Air, MD.

Winbrow, Thomas D. *If We Don't Have It, We'll Get It Wednesday: An Informal History of Courtland Hardware*. Bel Air, MD: Town of Bel Air Historic Preservation Collection, December 2001.

Wright, C. Milton. Oral History Interview, May 12, 1972. Harford County Public Library. Bel Air, MD.

Newspapers

Aegis. "Contract Let for Bel Air Post Office." July 31, 1936.

———. "Interior of New Post Office Is Most Pleasing." July 9, 1937.

———. "Many Lots Are Offered as Bel Air Post Office Sites." November 30, 1934.

———. "Mechanization with Unique Record Praises New Post Office Building Here." April 23, 1937.

———. "Post Office Bids High." July 24, 1936.

———. "Post Office Is Due $245,000 Improvements." October 19, 1961.

Aegis and Intelligencer. "The Bullett Carriage Factory." March 29, 1889.

———. "The Bullett Factory Burned." September 25, 1891.

———. "Business Index of the Foremost Lawyers, Bankers, Merchants, Manufacturers, Etc." November 11, 1887.

———. "The Good Samaritan Drug Store." November 12, 1880.

Afro-American. "Famous Harford County Horseman Dies." October 8, 1927.

Baltimore Sun. "Bullett Carriage Company." January 16, 1889.

———. "Bullett Carriage Company." June 19, 1891.

———. "Mr. Williams at Home." October 5, 1903.

———. "Positive Closing Out Sale of the Entire Stock." June 13, 1893.

———. "Staging by Automobiles." April 16, 1905.

Democratic Ledger. "Bel Air News." Saturday, April 3, 1897.

Reckord. "Mary Hall—A Native of Bel Air and Proud of the Past." July 24, 1974.

———. "Obituary of Warrenell Lester: Warrenell F. Lester, Boxer, Dies." April 11, 2004.

ABOUT THE AUTHOR

Carol Deibel served as the director of planning and community development for the Town of Bel Air for twenty-six years, developing the town's first historic preservation program and overseeing development as the town grew from a small rural community to a major suburban center. This experience placed her in a unique position to document the history of this community. Ms. Deibel is co-editor of Marilynn M. Larew's book, *Bel Air: An Architectural and Cultural History, 1782–1945*; editor of the Historical Society of Harford County, Inc. bimonthly newsletter; and author of several publications and articles for the Town of Bel Air, the Historical Society of Harford County and several local boards and commissions. She is currently working on an oral history project with the Harford County Historic Preservation Commission, collecting stories from Harford County residents about their lives and experiences in twentieth-century Harford County.

Visit us at
www.historypress.net